WALKING THE GALLOWAY HILLS

WALKING THE GALLOWAY HILLS

35 WILD MOUNTAIN WALKS INCLUDING THE MERRICK

by Ronald Turnbull

JUNIPER HOUSE, MURLEY MOSS,
OXENHOLME ROAD, KENDAL, CUMBRIA LA9 7RL
www.cicerone.co.uk

© Ronald Turnbull 2019
First edition 2019
ISBN: 978 1 78631 010 1
Reprinted 2025 (with updates)

Printed in Singapore by KHL printing on responsibly sourced paper.
A catalogue record for this book is available from the British Library.

© Crown copyright and database rights 2019 OS AC0000810376
All photographs are by the author unless otherwise stated.

*This book is dedicated with thanks to Andy Priestman
and his family, who first led me into the Galloway Hills.*

Updates to this guide

While every effort is made by our authors to ensure the accuracy of guidebooks as they go to print, changes can occur during the lifetime of an edition. Any updates that we know of for this guide will be on the Cicerone website (www.cicerone.co.uk/1010/updates), so please check before planning your trip. We also advise that you check information about such things as transport, accommodation and shops locally. Even rights of way can be altered over time. We are always grateful for information about any discrepancies between a guidebook and the facts on the ground, sent by email to updates@cicerone.co.uk.

Register your book: To sign up to receive free updates, special offers and GPX files where available, create a Cicerone account and register your purchase via the 'My Account' tab at www.cicerone.co.uk.

Front cover: Reaching the summit of Mullwarchar above Loch Enoch (Route 16)

CONTENTS

Map key 6

INTRODUCTION 8
Harshness and heather 9
Geology of the Galloway Hills 10
Wildlife and wet. 15
Free Forest of Buchan 17
Forest park and biosphere. 18
Climbing and scrambling 19
When to walk. 20
Getting here, getting around, staying the night 21
Maps and GPS 22
Safety in the hills 22
Using this book 24

SECTION 1: GLEN TROOL. 25
Route 1   Water of Minnoch and Glen Trool. 27
Route 2   Water of Trool 32
Route 3   Around Loch Trool 35
Route 4   Fell of Eschoncan to Bennan 39
Route 5   Merrick and Rig of the Buchan 43
Route 6   The Three Lochs 49
Route 7   Craignaw. 55
Route 8   Craiglee and Rig of the Jarkness. 60
Route 9   Mulldonoch to Curleywee 64
Route 10   Caldron of the Merrick 70

SECTION 2: THE AWFUL HAND 74
Route 11   Kirriereoch Hill and Merrick 76
Route 12   The Awful Hand: Shalloch to Benyellary 81
Route 13   Shalloch on Minnoch 87
Route 14   Craigmasheenie and Shiel Hill 91

SECTION 3: LOCH DOON 95
Route 15   Craiglee of Doon. 97
Route 16   Hoodens Hill and Mullwharchar 101
Route 17   Northern Rhinns of Kells from Loch Doon. 108

SECTION 4: THE GLENKENS 113
Route 18 Garryhorn and the northern Rhinns of Kells. 115
Route 19 Cairnsmore of Carsphairn 119
Route 20 Craig of Knockgray 124
Route 21 Corserine from Forrest Lodge. 128
Route 22 Southern Rhinns of Kells 133
Route 23 Mulloch Hill 137
Route 24 Waterside Hill. 140
Route 25 Dunveoch 143

SECTION 5: TALNOTRY AND THE SOUTH 146
Route 26 Larg Hill to Curleywee 148
Route 27 Curleywee by Stronbae Hill. 152
Route 28 Millfore 156
Route 29 Cairnsmore of Fleet from the north 160
Route 30 Cairnsmore of Fleet from the south 165
Route 31 Clints of Dromore 168
Route 32 Knockman Wood 174
Route 33 The Thieves Stones 178
Route 34 Wood of Cree 182

SECTION 6: EXPEDITIONS 185
Route 35 Not the Southern Upland Way 187
          Other routes 192

Appendix A   Route summary table 196
Appendix B   The bothies. 200
Appendix C   Information points 202

Route symbols on OS map extracts
(for OS legend see printed OS maps)

  route   start/finish point

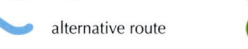 alternative route   start point

  route direction   finish point

                                         alternative start/finish point

GPX files for all routes can be downloaded free at www.cicerone.co.uk/1010/GPX.

Grey Man of the Merrick (Route 6)

INTRODUCTION

> In the wilds of Galloway that look towards Ayrshire, up by the springs of Doon and Dee, there lies a wide country of surpassing wildness, whither resorted all the evil gypsies of the hill – red-handed men, outlaws and aliens of all this realm of well-affected men.
> *SR Crockett, The Raiders*

> I fixed on Galloway as the best place to go
> *John Buchan, The Thirty-Nine Steps*

So maybe you're not a bandit or a red-handed man or lass. Maybe you aren't on the run from a gang of unseemly foreigners in the dark days before World War I, or Aymer de Valence and the English army in 1307. Even so, the Galloway Hills – the Galloway Highlands, as they used to be called – have a lot to offer to the more rugged sort of hillgoer. There are the grey boulders, the black peaty bog, the tussocks of grass. There are great slabs of naked granite, and two dozen sparkling lochs and lochans; long grassy ridges, and intricate wee hills like Craignaw and Curleywee.

The Galloway Hills are small, but special. They stretch just 20km (15 miles) from west to east, and 40km (25 miles) north to south – almost as

Minnigaff Hills from Benyellary (Route 5)

small as Snowdonia. Within that area – much of it pathless – Galloway has 23 summits over 2000ft, including four Corbetts (2500-footers).

Most of the summits line themselves into the three ridges around the edge. The Minnigaffs, the Rhinns of Kells and the Range of the Awful Hand give enjoyable grassy going and great views. But what those views are of – that's the bit in the middle. It's the bit where the wild goats go, and the legendary brigands of the untamed 17th century, and the grim-faced guerrilla warriors of Robert the Bruce.

If you like your wild landscape really wild... If you like your lakes to have whooper swans in the middle and no ice-cream vans around the edge... If you like to have one foot on bare rock and the other one deep in a peat bog... If you like your granite with goats on... Then Galloway is the place to go.

HARSHNESS AND HEATHER

The high ground of Galloway is rugged, remote, and rather different from anywhere you've been before. And it's wonderful country. However, those grassy ridgelines and that granite heartland do come at a cost. Much of the lower ground is unpathed, ungrazed, and poorly drained. Rather a lot of it is planted with dreary Sitka spruce. Much of the open moorland below the 300m level is heather, burnt down for grouse or luxuriating to the level of the hillwalker's thighs. Other low ground is tussocky grass, which, in August, can flourish almost as deep as the heather, with wet peaty holes between the tufts. Forest rides – the strips of rough grass between plantation blocks – sometimes have quad-bike wheelmarks but more often are the worst of grassy tussocks. Where drainage breaks down, there will be occasional wee peaty swamps.

GALLOWAY AND ITS HILLS

The ancient realm of Galloway stretches from the River Nith and Dumfries all the way down to Scotland's southwest corner at the Mull of Galloway. This includes many rounded, grassy hills that can be called 'ordinary Southern Uplands'. The name Galloway Hills, or Galloway Highlands, is reserved for the highest part of this hill ground: the self-contained and rocky patch between the River Minnoch and the Glenkens valley, stretching southwards to Cairnsmore of Fleet. Mostly contained within Dumfries & Galloway Region, at Loch Doon it runs down into Ayrshire.

This book covers these Galloway Hills, along with (on the eastern side of the Glenkens valley) Cairnsmore of Carsphairn, which is one of Galloway's four Corbetts (2500-footers) and shares the area's distinctive granite rocks.

WALKING THE GALLOWAY HILLS

Mental preparedness is everything. It helps to know in advance that the wonderful rocky ridgeline of Hoodens Hill (Route 16) must be paid for at day's end with a lot of forest road and a few hundred metres of nasty forest rides. So each walk is graded for harshness, as below.

Approaches from Loch Trool are not only very beautiful but also reasonably easy going. Elsewhere, some small paths are starting to form, and where these do exist (Shalloch from the north, Corserine from the east) I have taken advantage of them.

Where a route is graded as 4 or 5, this applies to its most demanding section, usually a short stretch on the approach or the walk-out. A high level of harshness is only justified where the main part of the walk is of especial excellence!

Harshness grading
1. Undemanding: smooth, well-surfaced and well-drained paths
2. Pleasant: rough hill paths, smooth grassy hilltops and ridges
3. Challenging: coarse grassland, bare granite slabs, steep stony paths
4. Hard: pathless heather, boggy coarse grassland, seriously steep slopes
5. Nasty: deep heather, deep grassy tussocks, bogs

GEOLOGY OF THE GALLOWAY HILLS

About 400 million years ago, what would eventually be called Scotland crunched into what would end up as England. On either side, the crumpled-up rocks formed the hill zones of today: the Highlands and the Lake District respectively. In between the two, deep-ocean sludges were raised and crumpled like a trodden-on tube of toothpaste. The crumpled sludges made a rock called greywacke; their hill range, in the squash zone between England and Scotland, is the Southern Uplands.

But Galloway got a hit of something different. As one continent burrowed underneath the other, underground heat melted the bedrock in great blobs of magma. These worked their way upwards, cooled and congealed into pale-grey, crystalline granite. One such lump of granite forms the distinctive heartland of the Galloways.

The granite, as it arrives, cooks and alters the surrounding greywacke rocks – this altered rock is called hornfels. And it's a bit like Goldilocks and the porridge. Far away, the granite heat has no effect. Right up against the granite, the cookery downgrades the greywacke into something crumbly. But in between, at a couple of kilometres out from the magma chamber, the greywacke gets hardened and improved.

Here in Galloway, the hornfels is tougher than the granite itself. And

Bluebells in Knockman Wood (Route 32)

Granite slabs on north ridge of Hoodens Hill (Route 16)

so, after erosion, the result is a ring of tough rocks – the Minnigaffs, the Rhinns of Kells and the Awful Hand – right around the granite hills of the Dungeon range in the middle. A ring of this sort, around a central granite nipple, is called a metamorphic areole. (The coastal hills of Screel and Bengairn, not included in this book, show the same formation in miniature.)

Greywacke

The unaltered greywacke rock is seen around the outer rim of the hills. It's a compact and featureless grey sandstone. The dull exterior conceals an exciting origin. In the deep ocean trench, nothing much happens for tens of thousands of years. But, thousands of metres above, mud and silt are slowly building up on the continental shelf. All of a sudden, this all slides down in an underwater avalanche, travelling at 100km/hr and sweeping away any trivial obstructions like undersea telephone cables.

Each mudslide becomes a single thick bed of greywacke. Where you can see them, the beds are usually standing on end or even upside down – the result of the Scotland–England collision that squashed and raised them. Being made of mud, the greywacke can be smooth and quite slippery, especially when wet.

Hornfels

The hardened and altered hornfels rocks, making the three hill ridges around the rim, are grey like the greywacke they started off as, but solid and knobbly. The heat of the arriving granite has allowed the original greywacke to partly crystallise. This welds it all together, and the crystal corners make for a rough and grippy rock. So the hornfels rocks can give satisfying scrambling.

GEOLOGY OF THE GALLOWAY HILLS

Granite

Granite cools slowly, deep underground in big lumps called plutons. As the pluton cools, it shrinks, cracking into big, regular blocks. The main shrinkage cracks are parallel with the top or side surfaces of the underground pluton. This means that granite at the top breaks into smooth, near-level slabs – as seen and walked on at Craignaw.

Because granite cools oh-so-slowly, it has time to form visible crystals several millimetres across. The crystals are of three sorts: tough, glassy quartz; white or grey feldspar; and a dark iron-rich mineral. The dark minerals and the feldspar rot away in the wind and rain, leaving the sharp-edged quartz standing proud to give a superbly grippy surface. This also results in rounding of the corners, giving a lack of actual handholds to climb with, but nicely rounded boulders decorating the hillsides. Meanwhile, the eroded-out quartz crystals form the pale, gleaming beaches of Loch Neldricken and Loch Enoch. It's a fair summary to say that what makes Galloway Galloway is the granite.

The ice

Finally came the ice ages, to give the hills their shapes of today. A deep ice cap was centred on Mullwharchar. Granite boulders from Mullwharchar and Craignaw, carried outwards by the ice, are seen on the surrounding ridges, and there's an obvious contrast where they've come to rest on the rather different hornfels rock. Bruce's Stone itself is one such.

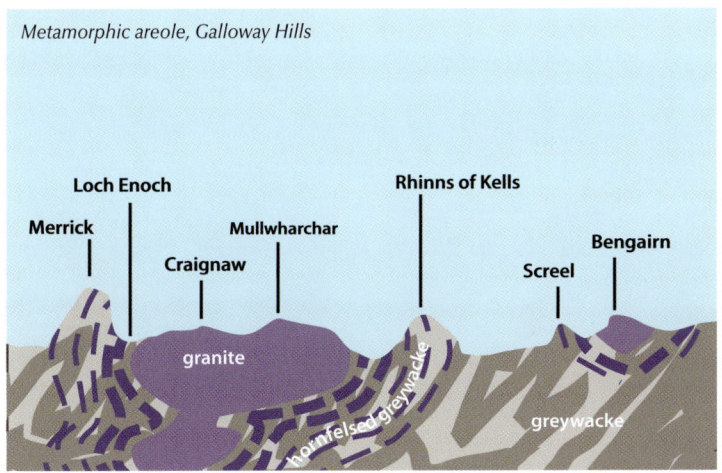

Metamorphic areole, Galloway Hills

Hornfels, with quartz veins; with Milldown, Rhinns of Kells (Route 22)

WILDLIFE AND WET

Interpretation boards at Cairnsmore of Fleet describe it as a high-altitude granite bog of international importance. That judgement is a little unkind – much of the ground is rock rather than bog. But these fairly low hills, with their mild, damp climate, do have a green and vigorous plant growth and the wildlife to match.

Around the southern edges of the range, the natural cover is Atlantic oakwood. Chunks of this lovely woodland remain, and these are being slowly infilled with the aim of creating a continuous natural wood right up the Cree valley to Glen Trool. These woods are at their best in late spring, with bluebells and other wildflowers. They are still a stronghold for the native red squirrel – but the invasive grey crossed the River Nith in 2018 and is likely to spread westwards, eliminating the red as it arrives. Roe deer also roam in these woodlands; your best chance of seeing them is if you're the first along a forest track very early in the morning.

Red kites were reintroduced into the Glenkens valley in 2001. They are now a common sight anywhere in Galloway, and at the feeding station at Bellymack, near Laurieston, you can see a dozen at once. The birds are general scavengers rather than hunting hawks. Roughly buzzard-sized but more slender, they can be recognised by their stubby-forked tails.

Among other raptors, buzzards are common, and peregrine, goshawk, sparrowhawk and merlin can sometimes be seen. Hen harriers appear to be extinct in this area, but a returning short-eared owl was spotted by the Galloway ranger in 2018 – unlike other owls, these fly and hunt by daylight. Up to three pairs of golden eagles nest, or have nested, in the Galloway Hills. The forlorn eagle that tried to inhabit the Lake District originated in Galloway. But if you're not sure what you've seen, then it was a buzzard – 99 per cent of reported eagle sightings are buzzards. If you're going 'What the heck is that? It's blooming huge!' – yes, that's an eagle.

In the granite heartland, the distinctive wildlife is the Galloway herd of wild goats. Technically, these are merely feral, as they're descended from domestic goats that have leapt over fences to freedom from the Bronze Age onwards. They have evolved wild, shaggy coats to withstand the Galloway rain. They're less often spotted than formerly, since some estate owners have started issuing hunting permits against them. However, some will normally be seen at the Wild Goat Park on the A712 at Talnotry, as this is their winter feeding station.

Red deer also roam the Galloway Hills. Your best chance of spotting them is at the Red Deer Range near Talnotry, or else on this book's less-used routes, in the unvisited corries on the outside of the three high ridges. I've met them on the southern flanks of the Minnigaffs and the western ones of the Awful Hand.

Loch Valley outflow (Route 7)

On warm, humid summer days, adders may occasionally be encountered on the lower slopes. The zigzag pattern on their backs is a sufficient warning not to play with snakes. Adders are shy and sensitive and keep clear when they can. If you (or, more likely, your dog) should chance to get bitten, then walk (not run) at a steady pace towards A&E in Dumfries or Ayr. Those who've experienced them say that adder bites, within a few hours, become very painful indeed, although human fatalities from adder bites are very rare.

Tucked away at the end of the wildlife, I ought to mention the three sorts of noxious insects met from early June to the first frost. The ubiquitous midge is as bad here as it is in the Highlands. Avoid it by staying high, choosing a breezy day, or keeping on the move. A midge bite, if you don't scratch it, fades in 15 minutes. But you do scratch, don't you? Former campsites in lush forest vegetation at Talnotry and Caldons were driven out of business by the midge – if camping, carry a midge net.

The evil cleg or horsefly bears the same ratio to the normal fly as the weasel does to the mouse – same general shape but twice as long. The cleg flies on hot, sultry days, and can chase down a walking human. If you see one on your flesh, gently squash it – a hard slap will drive the poison in. Otherwise the defence is to wear long sleeves and head up onto high ridges.

Lush vegetation, especially when wet, harbours the vile tick, which I just wrongly classed as an insect. It's actually an arachnid, with eight horrid little legs rather than six. Ticks leap off the leaves as you brush by, and crawl around until they find a cosy corner of your body such as an armpit or waistband. There, they attach themselves and start sucking blood. Unfortunately, they may occasionally return the favour by injecting the malignant Lyme disease. Apart from long sleeves and staying away in summer, there's nothing for it but careful inspection and removal. If a distinctive red 'target' rash appears around the tick bite, show it to your doctor.

Herbal repellents are fairly effective against midges, clegs and ticks, and chemical repellents somewhat more so.

GALLOWAY NAMES

Aobh cumar an eas dom,
Aobh bealach nan slògh
(Pleasant is the confluence of the waterfalls to me / Pleasant the pass of the hosts)
from *Òran Bagraidh*, the only known text in Gallovidian

Galloway is where Gaelic, Cumbric, Scots and Norse are all bubbling together in the Caldron of the Merrick. The name Galloway itself, from *Gall-Gaidhel*, means Norse–Gael. Carrick, the northwestern corner, is Old Irish *Carraig*, meaning rocky.

The last native speaker of the Gallovidian language may have been Alexander Murray, who died in 1813 (see Route 28). Although the language was closer to Manx than to Highland Gaelic, those familiar with the names of the north will recognise Kirriereoch as *Coire Riabhach*, the speckled corrie, and the common prefix Mull as *Meall*, a humpy hill. Gairy, the local name for a steep, craggy slope, seems to be from Gaelic *garadh*, which means a garden, but also one specific feature of a Highland garden, the high stone wall surrounding it. Dow Loch (two of those) is *Dubh Loch*, or black lake.

But really it's best just to relax and enjoy them: the Rig of the Jarkness, the Point of the Snibe, the Dungeon of Buchan and the Neive of the Spit. By the time you've covered Route 31, you'll have a fair idea of what a clint could be.

FREE FOREST OF BUCHAN

The history of the area starts, as histories should, with the Bronze Age. Those early tree-fellers and field cultivators left a few standing stones and a distinctive sort of chambered cairn: two or three tiny stone rooms, covered in a truly huge pile of stones, up to 10 metres across (see Routes 1, 32 and 33).

Skip to 1307, when Robert the Bruce, having foully murdered the puppet king of Scotland in a church at Dumfries, had no way forward from that situation other than going for the Crown himself. He established a small guerrilla force in the Galloway Hills. A very minor victory at Clatteringshaws Loch led to more followers and a slightly less minor victory at Glen Trool. In between times, he was hunted through the hills with his own bloodhounds.

Each successive victory increased his credibility and his following, culminating in beating the invading English in a full army battle at Bannockburn near Stirling in 1314 and the Crown of Scotland. In gratitude for the help received, he granted the hill people of Galloway and South Ayrshire the Free Forest of Buchan. On this royal hunting preserve, the scattered inhabitants had the right not to be oppressed by any nobles at all apart from himself as king.

In the late 17th century, King Charles II attempted to reimpose bishops on the Scottish Church. The hardline Protestants called Covenanters held illegal church services (conventicles) in all the hills of southern Scotland, including these ones. Their Pentland Rising against the Edinburgh government, in 1666, started at Dalry (see Route 23); it marked the start of an active and vicious persecution known as the Killing Times. The hills again became a refuge; here, the Covenanters' main memento is at Caldons (Route 2).

On into the Victorian period, small outlaw bands are reputed to have lurked here, with the Macaterick clan giving their name to a hill and one of the lochs. The Galloway Hills then became a range for the tough-as-granite Scotch Blackface sheep. Howlingly lonely shepherd's cottages were dotted through the hills – the access to Backhill of Bush was over the top of the Kells range. As late as the 1920s, the occasional hillwalker or tramp would get a cosy welcome at a shepherd's cottage. A handful of them remain as bothies, the rest lie in ruins among the heather or under the wood-pulp plantations.

FOREST PARK AND BIOSPHERE

In 2024, Galloway (including these hills and the region's entire coastline) was nominated by the Scottish Government as Scotland's third National Park. This starts a process of consultation that may (or may not) end up with formal designation. In the meantime, the whole of the Galloway

Heath spotted orchid

Bog asphodel

Goats on Craignaw, with Loch Enoch (Route 7)

Hills is designated as forest park. The land is mostly owned and managed by Forestry and Land Scotland, who have undertaken not to raise plantations on the best of the wild heartland around the 'three lochs', as well as all the high ridges, leaving them as open ground for the walker. Sadly, the outer slopes of the Awful Hand and the Minnigaffs, and lower slopes on both sides of the Rhinns of Kells range, remain as managed wood-pulp factories.

Cairnsmore of Fleet is a nature reserve, managed by Scottish Natural Heritage to conserve its special qualities as a high-level granite bog.

'Biosphere' is a United Nations designation conveying a particular effort of local involvement in the environment – it has no planning implications or special restrictions. The Galloway and Southern Ayrshire Biosphere stretches from Loch Ryan and Stranraer to Kirkcudbright and the Nith valley.

The Galloway sessile oakwoods, seen at Loch Trool and the Wood of Cree, form a Special Area of Conservation, representing the Southwest Lowlands Atlantic Bryophyte zone. (Bryophytes are liverworts and other primitive plants.)

Finally, while Galloway's peaty bits are blacker, so too are its night skies. The Galloway Hills constitute Scotland's first Dark Sky Park, unpolluted with light from habitations within the area or any large settlements nearby. Aspiring astronomers should note that, due to the area's high rainfall, those skies are quite often clouded over.

CLIMBING AND SCRAMBLING

The clean, rain-washed rocks of Galloway offer the occasional tiny crag to the scrambler, although these can always be walked around. No walk here will have scrambling as its primary purpose, but it's a bonus for those who want it on Buchan Hill (Route 6), Craiglee of Dee (Route 8), Mulldonoch (Route 9) and even little Dunveoch at St John's Town of Dalry (Route 25).

WALKING THE GALLOWAY HILLS

For climbers, the Galloways offer some short but steep climbs on good granite. The Tauchers of Mullwharchar and the Dungeon of Buchan are remote; the approaches are long; and the crag foot is reached through the toughest of tussocks, and, in the case of the Dungeon, the quaking bogs of the dreaded Silver Flowe.

The climbs are on the steep eastern faces of Mullwharchar, Dungeon Hill and Cairnsmore of Fleet. The guidebook is the Scottish Mountaineering Club's *Lowland Outcrops*; some route updates can be found on the website of the Keswick climber's shop, Needle Sports (www.needlesports.com), or on the SMC website (www.smc.org.uk). Access may be restricted during eagle nesting season. In winter, the north face of Merrick can offer informal routes at Grade I or II. Ambitious walkers can also enjoy the Caldron of the Merrick (Route 10) under snow and ice.

WHEN TO WALK

The notes above on nasty wee beasties and on the vegetation of the lower ground may have suggested that high summer, July and August, is not the ideal time to visit the Galloway Hills. August is also, in average years, the second wettest month. Even then, though, the high ridgelines are a delight; and the heather will be in flower.

However, the spring and early summer are the very best time, along with the early autumn months of September and October. These can often bring mild days with light breezes and 100km views.

Any month of the year can, also, bring low cloud and rain. This is western Scotland, and while the hills are smaller and slightly less serious, the weather is much the same as in the Scottish Highlands.

For those prepared to seek out the good days and tough out the bad ones, winter can be a superb walking season. Very heavy snowfalls are unusual

Loch Trool from the path to Loch Valley (Routes 6–8)

GETTING HERE, GETTING AROUND, STAYING THE NIGHT

Lagwine Cairn (Route 20)

– although in spring 2018 I did observe the debris of an avalanche on the east slope of Shalloch on Minnoch. In mountains further north, we hope for the freeze-and-thaw cycle to firm up the snow. Galloway tends to thaw-and-thaw – so don't expect perfect conditions, and adjust your plans. And you'll find winter in Galloway has a wild beauty that's very hard to match. There might even be ice on Loch Enoch to walk over (at your own risk!) to visit the Loch in the Loch.

GETTING HERE, GETTING AROUND, STAYING THE NIGHT

The unpopulated Galloway Hills are not well served by public transport. Cairnsmore of Fleet (Route 30) can be accessed directly from Newton Stewart, along with lower-level Route 32. There are buses (Stagecoach 359) to Bargrennan and Glen Trool for the low-level Route 1. And in the east, the Glenkens bus 520 runs between Dalmellington, St John's Town of Dalry and Castle Douglas five times a day (less at weekends), giving direct access to the hills at Carsphairn (Routes 18–20) and shorter walks at St John's Town of Dalry. Otherwise, none of the walks is reached by bus or train.

Walkers without cars who are of rugged disposition can explore the main hill area using the bothies. You can walk in to these from various access points, and explore the entire range over about five days. Suggested walk-in and walk-out routes along with details of the bothies themselves are in Appendix B.

It remains the case that almost everyone walking in the Galloway Hills is making their final approach by car. Those travelling here by air should aim for Glasgow International 1½hr to the north; you could take a train to Ayr and hire a car there. Travelling within the UK, take a train to Dumfries, where a car can be hired at the railway station.

Granite boulder at Merrick summit (Route 5) shows that the glacier came right over the top

MAPS AND GPS

The best map for detailed exploration of the area is the Harvey 1:25,000 *Galloway Hills*, republished in 2019. As well as being superbly clear and legible, and printed on tough, waterproof plastic, it marks paths and forest rides (tree gaps) where they actually are. This map can be purchased in electronic form onto smartphones via the OutdoorActive app – with the disadvantage that you can't then use it as an emergency groundsheet.

The Ordnance Survey Explorer® maps are at the same scale and also show paths and forest rides. The difference is that these do not always correspond with what's on the ground (don't try and find their path from Culsharg to Loch Enoch). Sheet 318 (*Galloway Forest Park North*) covers the Galloway Hills north of the Southern Upland Way; Sheet 319 (*Galloway Forest Park South*) covers Cairnsmore of Fleet and the Minnigaffs, with Loch Trool appearing usefully on both maps. Sheet 328 (*Sanquhar & New Cumnock*) covers Cairnsmore of Carsphairn.

This book uses OS Landranger® mapping at 1:50,000 scale; the relevant sheet is 77 (*Dalmellington & New Galloway*), which also covers Cairnsmore of Carsphairn and the not-altogether-boring Windy Standard range to the northwest.

GPX tracks

GPX tracks for the routes in this guidebook are available to download free at www.cicerone.co.uk/1010/GPX. These files are provided in good faith, but neither the author nor the publisher accept responsibility for their accuracy.

SAFETY IN THE HILLS

Although they lack spectacular crags, these hills should be considered as

SAFETY IN THE HILLS

a step more serious than the Lake District or Snowdonia, and roughly on a par with the Scottish Highlands or remotest parts of the Pennines. Paths are sketchy and some of the low ground is extremely tough. Rivers may be uncrossable; forest plantations may give shelter but are also very troublesome to force a way through. For the more ambitious routes in this book, walkers need to be reasonably fit, well equipped for the season, and, above all, competent in finding their way around. I deliberately do not supply a 'suggested kit' list. If you need kit suggestions, then you probably aren't experienced enough to tackle the more serious routes here.

The three high ridges (Minnigaffs, Awful Hand and Rhinns of Kells) as well as the two Cairnsmores have mobile phone coverage on the whole, but the heartland in the middle mostly does not. In emergency, dial 999 (which will connect you via any network, not just your own) and ask for Police Scotland and then for Mountain Rescue.

Holm Wood (Route 1)

Rhinns of Kells seen from Shalloch (Route 13)

WALKING THE GALLOWAY HILLS

Below the Caldron of the Merrick (Route 10)

USING THIS BOOK

If the way to use this book isn't self-explanatory, then I and Cicerone haven't done it right... A box at the start of each route description provides key information about the route, including (where appropriate) a 'Variants' section explaining how, and why, you might shorten or lengthen the route. Each route is graded 1–5 for harshness: see 'Harshness and heather' above.

In Appendix A, a route summary table lists variants as well as main routes, to help you find something the length you'd like at the various starting points. Appendix B gives details of bothies and their access routes; and there's a list of contact information in Appendix C.

GPX tracks are available from the Cicerone website to buyers of this book. While the book's mapping, perhaps in conjunction with mapping in a smartphone or GPS, should get you around each of the routes, it is unwise not to also have one of the paper maps suggested above for when you stray off the route or need an emergency way off to the little Straiton road.

Equipped with map, waterproofs, and even, perhaps, some sunscreen, you'll find these hills, wild as the Highlands but enjoyably small, have a shaggy character all their own.

Oh the Gallowa' hills are covered wi' broom,
Wi' heather bells in bonnie bloom,
Wi' heather bells an' rivers a'
An' I'll gang o'er the hills tae Gallowa'

Traditional Scottish song (original version William Nicholson early 19th century)

SECTION 1: GLEN TROOL

Murder Hole, Loch Neldricken (Route 6)

SECTION 1: GLEN TROOL

Glen Trool, *Gleann an t-Sruthail*, is the Glen Of The Running Streams. It could equally well have been the Glen Of The Oakwoods, or the Glen Of The Rocky Slopes. But if you go along with the Gaelic tradition of giving humdrum names to the loveliest of places, it would have to be the Glen With The Loch In It. You walk under the trees from the road-end car parks to the nearby Bruce's Stone to find yourself high above the water in one of the most stunning spots in southern Scotland.

Already behind you at that point are long but gentle walks through the woodlands and along the peaty rivers (the linked Routes 1 and 2). An even better one (Route 3) leads right around the loch. And the Southern Upland Way's dirt track heads out around the base of the Minnigaff range. Meanwhile, beside you, a well-made path runs up onto southern Scotland's highest summit, the Merrick, at 843m – not that far under the Munro height of 3000ft. The route there (Route 5) is no mere uphill plod, but a swinging high-level ridgeline over Benyellary.

And yet, all this is just Galloway's gentler face. Across the loch, it's very obvious that Mulldonoch is an altogether different sort of ground, bristling with small rocky knolls. That hill, once you've found the hidden old pathway through its defending trees, makes the start of a route line (Route 9) that switches mood abruptly along the airy ridge of Lamachan Hill that rises behind.

And what you see over on Mulldonoch is only the start of it. A rough, but very romantic, way leads steeply up onto Fell of Eschoncan (Route 4). Routes 6 and 7 lead in to Loch Enoch and Craignaw, the Galloway heartland of sparkling lochans, bare granite and occasional black peaty bits.

If you only come to these hills once, then you'll come to Glen Trool. But having come to Glen Trool, you'll surely be inspired to come to Galloway many times again. Or almost surely… One Aymer de Valence and his small army probably thought once was quite enough after being speared to death by Robert the Bruce all along the wooded lochside slopes.

So it's not surprising that Loch Trool is the standard start point for days in the Galloway Hills. Other entry points are available. But all things being equal, Glen Trool is the one to go for.

ROUTE 1
Water of Minnoch and Glen Trool

Start/finish	River Minnoch near Clachaneasy (NX 362 749)
Alternative Start/finish	Stroan Bridge (NX 372 785) or Bargrennan at River Cree (NX 349 764)
Distance	13km (8 miles)
Ascent	200m (600ft)
Harshness	1
Approx time	3hr 30min
Terrain	Good paths
Highest point	White Cairn, 120m
Parking	Turn off A714 at Clachaneasy, in 800 metres turn right, in another 800 metres reach a crossing forest track; parking 50 metres down track to left. More parking just across River Minnoch up short, unsigned track on left.
Variants	See Route 2

Galloway Hills are not, on the whole, an easy place to be. But this walk is. It uses a long stretch of the waymarked and maintained Southern Upland Way (SUW), alongside the three rivers of Cree, Minnoch and Trool, and through some ancient oakwoods. Halfway around, there's a snack stop at Stroan Bridge, and on the return there's the area's most impressive chambered cairn.

The only downside (apart from the absence of hills) is the 2km of road walking into Bargrennan. New for 2019 is a well made and very welcome roadside footpath between Glentrool village and the House o' Hill in Bargrennan.

From the parking pull-off, continue northeast along the track. After 800 metres, the waymarked SUW path forks off right. It runs near **Water of Minnoch** then in scrubby woodland and clearings in plantations, mostly felled but with some high stands of pine and spruce.

After 1km the path rejoins the river, which may be heard before seen. Here, a waymark in the bracken

WALKING THE GALLOWAY HILLS

indicates a left bend in the path, but take the smaller path ahead. It bends right, following the riverbank downstream to the **Roman Bridge**.

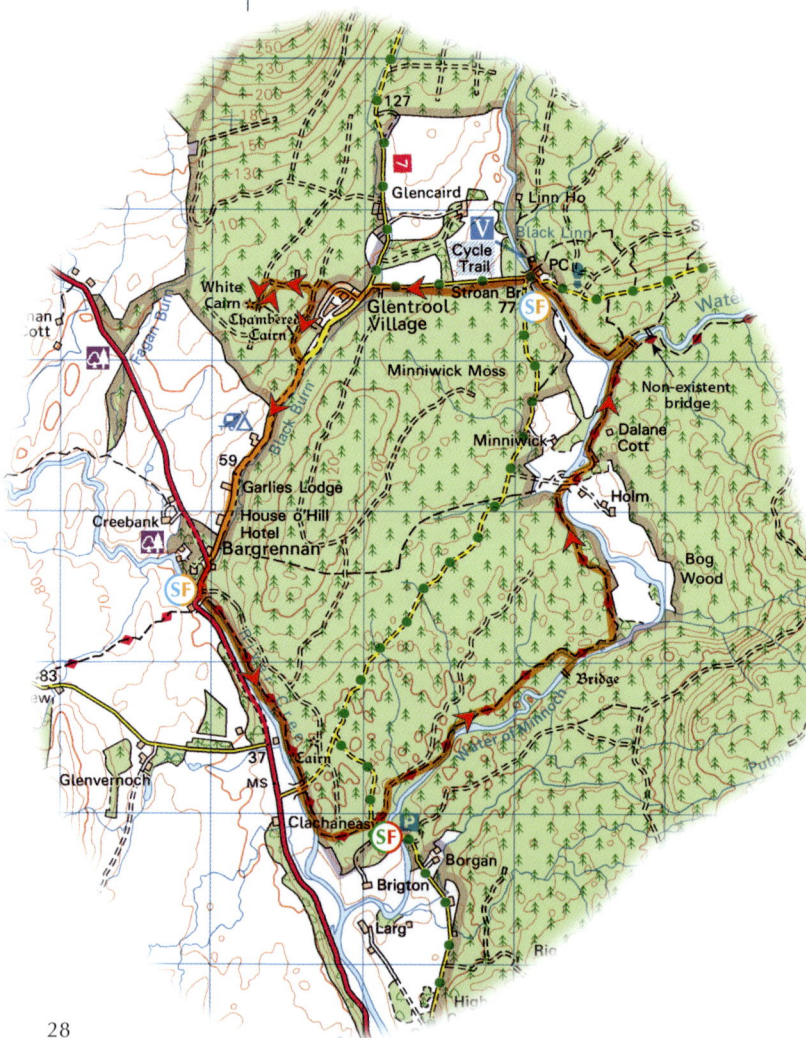

Roman Bridge, Water of Minnoch

The so-called **Roman Bridge** is actually a medieval packhorse bridge (or possibly even newer than that). It's a spectacular high arch above a narrows of the Water of Minnoch, and has survived storm spates that have demolished most of the more recent bridges at one time or another.

Return, and continue northeast on the main path, soon with a step stile over a wall dividing Brigton and Holm Woods. Through tall oak trees, the path reaches Holm Bridge.

Cross and turn left, on a faint path, through one small gate then with a fence on your left to another gate. Soon the path joins the riverbank and follows it upstream. A bench marks the point where Minnoch and Trool join. The path continues alongside **Water of Trool** for 400 metres to reach a noticeboard with path map and a high footbridge over Trool. ▶

The upper footbridge shown on the map doesn't exist. For Route 2 to Caldons and Loch Trool, stay to the right of the river on the SUW.

Cross and turn left on a wide, well-made gravel path. It runs through woods near the Trool then joins the Minnoch to follow it upstream, with a waterfall just before arriving at the car park beside **Stroan Bridge** (alternative Start/finish).

Cross the rebuilt road bridge, then ignore a road on the left (a shortcut south back to Clachaneasy). In a few more steps, fork left on a path signed for Glentrool Village. This good path runs in woods which hide the nearby road. It rejoins the road briefly to cross a small bridge, then heads back into woods, bending left to emerge at the edge of **Glentrool Village**.

A few steps ahead, bear up right into the village. ◄ As the street bends left, a narrow path on the right, with a white waymark, starts opposite a sign forbidding golf play. A small path through cleared forestry soon meets a rough track not marked on maps. Turn left on this, at once bending right to meet a clearer track. Follow this left for 50 metres, to a small path through bracken up on the right.

At the time of writing, the village has no shop or facilities.

This runs to meet another forest track. Turn left for 200 metres, to a track T-junction in plantations. Turn left again, to an info board on the right where the **White Cairn chambered cairn** is just inside the plantations.

WHITE CAIRN

This is the best example you'll see of the Bargrennan type of chambered cairn, a Bronze Age structure that's probably a tomb. It consisted of a small tunnel passageway built of stone slabs, buried within a cairn or stonepile 15 metres wide. Here at the White Cairn, enough of the overlying stones have been removed (probably for wall building) to expose the tunnel structure and the passageway leading to it.

This is the best preserved of a dozen similar cairns in the neighbourhood, two more being seen on Routes 32 and 33.

White Cairn chambered cairn

Route 1 – Water of Minnoch and Glen Trool

Return to the track, and follow it back left for 20 metres. Now there's a path forking right at a waymark post. If the path is not overgrown, follow it through clearfell northeast past a picnic table and down to rejoin the track on the arrival route. Follow this to the right, then the small path down right, to rejoin the track near the edge of Glentrool Village. Turn right, south. The track bends left to reach the two-lane road south of Glentrool Village. ▶

This track is not a designated trail, and could be closed for forest operations, in which case backtrack to Glentrool Village.

Turn right, along the quite busy road, but with a fine, wide footpath, first to its right and then to its left, as far as the **House o' Hill**. Bear left on the A714 across a small river. Pass across a large parking area (alternative Start/finish) to a SUW signpost just before the bridge over River Cree. Across a stile over the crash barrier, the path runs beside the river, then in the edge of pine plantations above. The going gets slightly soggy, then the path reaches the back road near **Clachaneasy**.

Cross slightly to the right, where the SUW path leads downstream in woods. After 400 metres, the main path turns up left away from the river – don't take a smaller path ahead through an old drystone wall. The path runs east, with the wall on its right to start with. It joins a track, which you follow to the right (no waymark) to reach another minor road. Cross to the parking pull-off at the walk start.

ROUTE 2
Water of Trool

Start/finish	Stroan Bridge (NX 372 785)
Alternative Start/finish	Caldons bridge (NX 396 790)
Distance	7km (4½ miles)
Ascent	150m (500ft)
Harshness	1
Approx time	2hr 15min
Terrain	Good paths
Highest point	Glen Trool, 160m
Parking	Pay-and-display at Stroan Bridge
Variants	If you start at Caldons, Stroan Bridge is well placed for a snack stop halfway round the walk. This route can be combined with Route 3 to give 16.5km (10½ miles) with 450m (1500ft) ascent – about 5hr. Runners could also add in Route 1 for 27.5km (17 miles) with 650m (2100ft) ascent on good fast paths – about 10hr.

The outward part of the walk passes through ground clear-felled in the 2010s and well up from the valley floor, so with wide views to the Minnigaff range and glimpses of Loch Trool. The return is alongside the slow-moving and gloomy Water of Trool. There's a waterfall on the way, and a handy café at the end. And for the energetic, it's the link in a sequence of paths between Bargrennan and the head of Loch Trool.

At the time of writing, the trail maps show this route as the Forestry Commission's yellow trail, but the waymarks take a slightly different line. All FC trails may get realigned from time to time, or re-waymarked in a different colour. Designated trails have the advantage that, even if closed for forest operations, a valid alternative will usually be signed.

At the walk start, don't be misled by various mountain bike trails starting out of the car park. Take the track towards the café for a few steps. Just before a stream bridge, turn up right on a tarmac path past signboards.

Route 2 – Water of Trool

The path becomes a wide gravel one. It crosses a bike path, and after 250 metres a forest track. Then it runs with a wall on its right to meet another forest track.

Turn left along the track. In 50 metres a wide path on the right is marked with all waymark colours (red, blue, yellow) but keep ahead along the track. ▶ After 800 metres, it forks – take the right fork, to shortcut across the loop of the left fork, which rejoins after passing the start of a bike path that we don't want. The rejoining tracks bend left and run to a wide turning circle. Directly ahead a path continues, uphill for the first few steps.

The path runs along the high side of Glen Trool, through ground mostly cleared of plantations, crossing a footbridge below a waterfall further up the slope. As you get glimpses of Loch Trool ahead, the path bends downhill in gentle zigzags. It runs through a clump of very tall spruce (probably to be felled around 2020) then zigzags again to arrive at the valley road.

Cross leftwards into the side lane to Caldons, signed to 'start of Loch Trool Trail', and follow it to a car park at **Caldons**. ▶ Keep ahead over **Water of Trool** by a bridge marked 'no access to vehicles'. In a few steps, turn right on the clear path of the Southern Upland Way (SUW), also with yellow trail waymarks. A notice about path flooding is on your left, and a SUW info board about the Battle of Glentrool

> The track is the yellow trail as marked on trail maps – the waymarking on the ground differs.

> Alternative Start/finish, and start of Route 3 around Loch Trool.

(Route 3) on your right. After 100 metres, some rock-composite surfboards are in the woods on the left. Then a short side path on the left leads to the **Martyr's Tomb**.

> In the Killing Times of the 1680s, the newly restored King Charles II tried to impose bishops on the staunchly Presbyterian churchgoers of southwest Scotland. Those who resisted, called **Covenanters**, held open-air services in the woods; their illicit ministers took refuge in the wilder hills, including these ones. The house which stood here at Caldons was where some worshippers were surprised and shot by government troops.

The path runs in woods, then alongside the slow-flowing **Water of Trool**. As the river starts to flow noisily in rocks, you reach a high footbridge. ◄ Cross it and turn left on a wide, well-made gravel path. This runs through woods near the Water of Trool then joins **Water of Minnoch** to follow it upstream. There's a waterfall on your left just before you arrive at the car park beside **Stroan Bridge**.

Route 1 arrives here from downstream. The upper footbridge shown on the map doesn't exist.

Southern Upland Way west of Caldons

ROUTE 3
Around Loch Trool

Start/finish	Caldons bridge (NX 396 790)
Distance	9.5km (6 miles)
Ascent	300m (1000ft)
Harshness	1
Approx time	3hr
Terrain	Good path, track, 1.5km of quiet road
Highest point	Bruce's Stone, 140m
Parking	Access lane to the former Caldons campsite, signed 'start of Loch Trool Trail'
Variants	Can combine with Route 2, starting at Stroan Bridge

Along with the ascent of the Merrick from Bruce's Stone, this circuit of Loch Trool is the only walk in the Galloway Hills that can be described as popular. And rightly so, given its combination of a good, waymarked path, beautiful ancient woodlands, the lake itself, and clear-felling in the early 2010s which has opened up wide views of the water and the hills opposite.

It's just a bonus that this is also the site of a small but significant victory of future king Robert the Bruce in 1307 – the path passes right through the ambush site and battlefield.

Take the tarmac track over **Water of Trool**. For a preliminary visit to the Martyr's Tomb (a memorial to the Covenanters – see Route 2), turn right with Southern Upland Way (SUW) markers to pass an info board about the battlefield. In 300 metres, the wide path has a short side path on the left to a walled enclosure around the **Martyr's Tomb**.

Return to the tarmac track. Keep ahead across the track (ignore SUW markers pointing to the right) onto a woodland path. This crosses a footbridge, turns upstream, then bends left for a glimpse of the foot of Loch Trool. The path then bends up right to rejoin, and turn left along, the SUW's tarmac track.

WALKING THE GALLOWAY HILLS

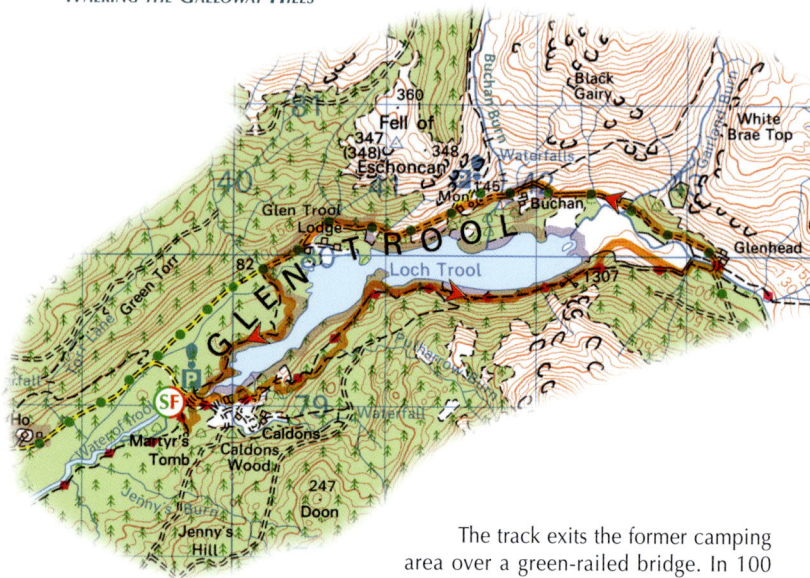

The track exits the former camping area over a green-railed bridge. In 100 metres, bear right on the main path, which climbs, soon beside a stream, to arrive high above Loch Trool. The path then descends almost to the lochside. Clear-felling of this slope, which is being replanted with native broadleaf trees, now provides grand views of the loch and the mountains above – Fell of Eschoncan, Buchan Hill, and a glimpse of the Merrick high behind. As it reaches the loch foot, the path climbs quite steeply, then descends gently – ignore a lesser path forking up right.

At the valley floor, the path joins Glenhead Burn and heads upstream to a track bridge near **Glenhead**. Turn left over the burn, and soon ignore a track back right for Glenhead. The main track ahead passes through ancient woodland, mostly oak, crosses Gairland Burn, and rises gently. ◄ The track crosses an old bridge over **Buchan Burn** and then rises steeply. As it bends sharply right, keep ahead in a rocky little path up to the Bruce's Stone (marked on the map as **Mon**) above Loch Trool.

Buchan house is hidden on the left, as is a small hydroelectric station which can be heard but not seen. The hydro scheme has snatched some of the waterfalls upstream.

ROBERT THE BRUCE

In 1306, Robert Bruce, Lord of Annandale, murdered one of his rivals in an especially inauspicious way, during a peace conference in Greyfriars Church at Dumfries. His only way out of the resulting political awkwardness was to seize for himself the Crown of Scotland, which at the time was going loose while Edward of England decided how best to bestow it.

He was quickly defeated, twice, by Edward's supporters, and fled to northern Ireland. In 1307 he returned with about 300 followers, to establish a safe base in this, the wildest country of his home ground of Galloway – the hills already familiar to him from deer-hunting in happier times.

In April 1307, an English army of about 1500 men came up into Galloway. Bruce attacked their camp alongside Clatteringshaws Loch (where there is a second Bruce's Stone). But this was merely a provocation, to lure them into chasing him along the narrow path on the south side of Loch Trool. Bruce himself coordinated the ambush from across Loch Trool, where his Stone now stands.

> Bot thai had standyn bot a thraw
> Rycht at thar hand quhen that thai saw
> Thar fayis throu the wod cummand
> Armyt on fute with sper in hand
> That sped thaim full enforcely.
> The noyis begouth sone and the cry
> *John Barbour, The Brus (c.1375)*

> They had no long time waiting stood / Before through the surrounding wood / They saw the Englishmen appear / Marching on foot with levelled spear. / Mightily onward came the foes / And soon loud battle shouts arose
> *Translation: Michael MacMillan, The Bruce of Bannockburn (1914)*

Large boulders came tumbling down the steepest part of the slope; any natural granite erratics, with their rounded shapes, will have been especially convenient. The stonefall was followed by a hail of arrows and then Bruce's lightly armed and agile fighters. The victory was small in numbers but significant; it started to persuade the Scots that England's Edward could be sent homeward to think again. Bruce's support now steadily increased, allowing slightly bigger victories and eventual defeat of the English at Bannockburn in 1314.

Bruce's Stone and Mulldonoch

Glenhead Wood

The wide path to the right leads to the upper car park, but go down behind the memorial to find a small path descending in woods to the lower car park. Follow the lane gently downhill through woods. As the road levels off, you pass the driveway for **Glen Trool Lodge** on your left. In another 250 metres, just after crossing a stream, turn left in a rough path – or keep on for a few steps to the more formal signposted path just ahead. The two soon join and cross the valley floor, felled ground with views. The path bends right to run close to the last narrow section of Loch Trool, then reaches the bridge at **Caldons**.

ROUTE 4

Fell of Eschoncan to Bennan

Start/finish	Bruce's Stone, upper car park (NX 415 804)
Distance	7.5km (4½ miles)
Ascent	450m (1500ft)
Harshness	4
Approx time	3hr 30min
Terrain	Small steep bracken path, small heather path, rough hillside and plateau; good path for descent
Highest point	Bennan, 562m
Parking	Two car parks at Bruce's Stone: the route starts from the higher one at the road's end
Variants	Short return by Culsharg bothy: 4.5km (2½ miles) with 250m (800ft) ascent – about 2hr. Continuation to Merrick (Route 5) and return to Route 4: 13.5km (8½ miles) with 850m (2800ft) ascent – about 5hr. Continuation to Merrick and onwards by Loch Enoch (Route 5 all the way): 14.5km (9½ miles) with 950m (3100ft) ascent – about 6hr.

Small but strenuous, the Fell of Eschoncan rises immediately above Bruce's Stone in steep bracken. The very small path was created with a strimmer for the first running of the Merrick hill race, to avoid some path-repairing works on the main Culsharg route. Over the years, the trainer-clad feet of the runners have kept the route open, although it is still very tricky to trace in high summer from July until the bracken gets squashed back on the mid-September race day.

Continuing over Bennan makes for a tough off-route route to Merrick or a shorter circuit in its own right. Bennan's top is surprisingly rocky and rugged for such a very flat place.

From the last parking bay on the left, and before the Merrick path, take a small indistinct path across a ditch and up the **Fell of Eschoncan**. ▶ The path heads through very thick bracken, directly uphill then with a short horizontal section to the right. With a rocky steepening

Many people pronounce this as Fell of Esconchan.

Minnigaff Hills from the slopes of Bennan

A little viewpoint cairn is about 50 metres southwest, overlooking the foot of Loch Trool.

For the shortcut, turn right down the forest road for 1km. The clear but unsigned path now turns down right to pass Culsharg bothy.

above, the path slants up to the right, passing just below two stray spruce trees, and rounds the corner of the hill to the east-facing slope.

This is the top of the bracken zone, with some clear-felled plantation just ahead. The path is easily lost just at this point (although if it is lost, the going is okay anyway). The path stays on the east flank above the lower Buchan Burn, heading up west to reach one of the summit cairns (348m). ◂ The path, now reasonably clear, passes to the right of the summit cairn and another cairn just beyond, and crosses a dip separating Fell of Eschoncan from the lower slopes of Bennan. A **trig point** is over on the left at this point. It isn't the summit – 1m too low – but does have views across the lowlands; if visiting it, return to the path. The path heads north, soon among some more escaped spruce trees, to reach a **forest road**. ◂

Cross the forest road to the corner of a deer fence, and go up to the right of the fence. As it bends right, there's a big escalator-style stile over it. (It's so helpfully constructed that the wild goats find it well convenient for access to the juicy broadleaf trees within.)

ROUTE 4 – FELL OF ESCHONCAN TO BENNAN

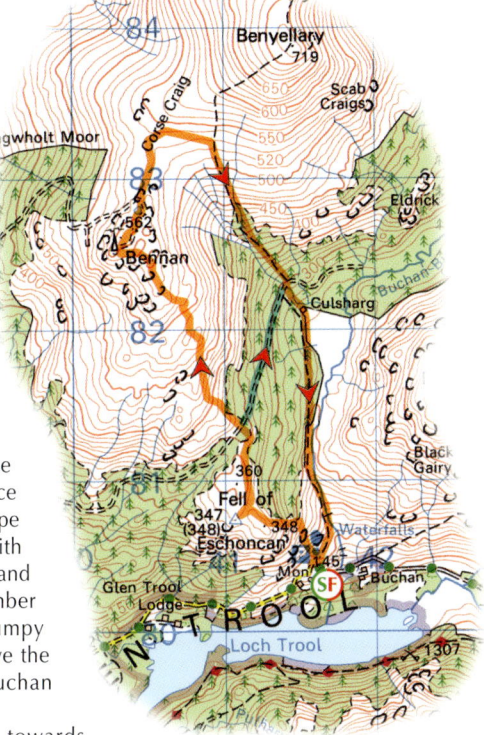

Keep uphill on the same line (northwest) as the lower fence was. Bamboos with orange tape mark the very small path, with tape presumably brightened and refreshed come mid-September race day. Slant up the bumpy slope to a cairn poised above the long slope down to the Buchan Burn.

Bear left, directly up towards **Bennan** (possibly still picking up bamboo markers), passing to the right of a tiny but beautiful pool and between the posts of a former fence to the wide, bumpy hilltop. The markers continue north, but bear northwest, towards the summit **radio mast**. The way is obstructed by tilted greywacke beds projecting from the moor, each with a slabby drop on the further side. So the going is interesting but slow, to reach the gravel road and Bennan's cairn just beyond the radio mast.

Head back northeast above the gravel road to cross the hill's true but unmarked summit, and rejoin the gravel road until it bends back left. Here, keep ahead to a tall ladder stile over the deer fence just ahead, and follow a faint grass track to a field gate in a wall. Through (or over) the gate, follow the wall to the left, then join a wall running back to the right – shortcutting this corner leads into soggy ground. Follow this new wall to the base of **Benyellary**. ◀

If continuing to Merrick, keep uphill by the wall to join Route 5.

Contour to the right along the base of the steeper ground to meet the clear descending path (rebuilt in chunky hardcore) to a gate in a deer fence. The path is rough as it runs downhill through recent (2015) clear-fell, to enter plantations over a marker stone for the woodland top. The path is very stony and somewhat eroded under the trees.

At a forest road, turn right for a few steps over a stream, then downhill on a clear path to pass the austere **Culsharg bothy**. Here, the path turns right and runs roughly level above Buchan Burn, through ground that was replanted in the mid 2010s. Peaty mud and rounded granite boulders make awkward walking for the last few steps down to the **car park**.

Bennan summit cairn

ROUTE 5
Merrick and Rig of the Buchan

Start/finish	Bruce's Stone, upper car park (NX 415 804)
Distance	13.5km (8½ miles)
Ascent	900m (2900ft)
Harshness	3
Approx time	5hr 30min
Terrain	Good path for ascent; rough grassy slopes and small path for descent
Highest point	Merrick, 843m
Parking	Two car parks at Bruce's Stone: the route starts from the higher one at the road's end
Variants	Route 4 offers a wilder ascent over Fell of Eschoncan and Bennan. The return leg of Route 6 also gives an excellent return to Bruce's Stone, while the energetic could even take in Craignaw (Route 7 reversed).

Big isn't always beautiful. But this route up the Merrick, highest point of southern Scotland, is a fine outing for reasons other than mere statistics. The start point at Loch Trool is very lovely, as well as having a historic rock commemorating Scottish independence and the battlefield across the loch (Route 3). The made-up path through the plantations is helpful, even if still somewhat rugged in places. But it's after Benyellary that the walk takes classic status, with its high-level ridge wander along the Neive of the Spit, looking into the granity heartland of Galloway and its many little lochs.

After the short wander east along the plateau for the view down to Loch Enoch, a return by the same route makes for a satisfying hill day, and one that is by Galloway standards notably low in ruggedness. But why see Loch Enoch when you could be at it? So this route continues down the Redstone Rig to that sublime central loch, before escaping along the fairly dry and easy ground of the Rig of the Buchan.

There's only one Merrick, and the hill is referred to locally as *The Merrick*. This is reflected on the larger-scale OS map only, at the point where the slope to the summit is named as Broads of the Merrick.

WALKING THE GALLOWAY HILLS

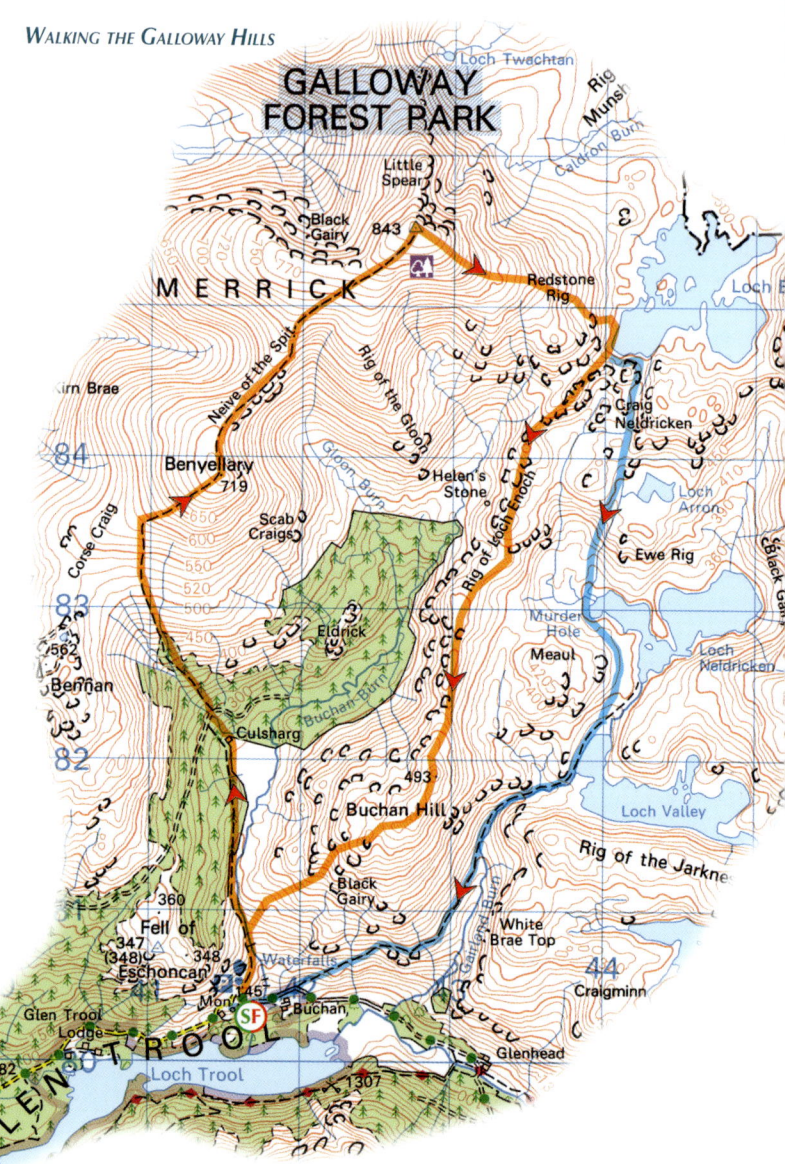

ROUTE 5 – MERRICK AND RIG OF THE BUCHAN

At the top end of the car park, a wide path sets off uphill (northeast) with a large signboard announcing it as the Merrick Trail. The path is rugged, with peat and boulders, but gets better higher up. In 200 metres, it arrives above the wooded slot of the **Buchan Burn**, with waterfalls heard below.

The path runs above the stream for about 400 metres, then turns uphill a little and contours through plantation that was felled and replanted in the mid 2010s. It is now wide and fairly smooth and will remain reasonably comfortable for the rest of the ascent. At **Culsharg bothy** (well restored in 2016, but by 2018 re-wrecked by vandals), the path turns uphill to a forest road. Turn right for 50 metres, crossing a stream, to find the path continuing uphill through a gate in deer fencing.

The path emerges over a carved stone marking the top of woodland, to pass through a gate onto open fellside and then reach the wall up the southwest flank of Benyellary. ▶ The path runs up to the right of the wall, to the large summit cairn of **Benyellary**.

Route 4 walkers arriving from Bennan would join here.

Here, the wall and path bend left, descending around the rim of the Gloon corrie onto the well-defined ridgeline **Neive of the Spit**. The path to the right of the wall follows the brink of the corrie; the path up to the left offers additional views westwards towards the sea and Ailsa Craig. At the end of this connecting ridge, the wall and path bend slightly left (north) up the summit slope of the **Merrick**. After 200 metres, the path bends right, away from the wall, to rake up the hill flank to the white-painted trig point.

VIEW FROM THE MERRICK

On a clear day, the sea is in sight over more than 180 degrees of the vista. Merrick's special location can give an overview of all the component parts of the UK (well, not the Channel Islands). Northwestwards are distinctive islands: the volcanic plug of Ailsa Craig; beyond it, the jagged outline of Arran; and on a good day the twin points of the Paps of Jura, just to the right of the Arran mountains. And on such a clear day, northwards across Glasgow will appear the Highlands, with Ben Lomond and Ben Lawers the most readily identifiable.

Heading to the Merrick along Neive of the Spit

Northeastwards lie the rounded humps of the Southern Uplands. Southeastwards may be seen the English Lake District. Southwards you might spot the Isle of Man, with its summit Snaefell. And further round lies Ireland, with the Mourne Mountains in the southwest and the Antrim hills due west.

But the real surprise, on an exceptionally clear day, is the UK's longest view. Look just to the left of the Isle of Man and immediately above Lamachan Hill: it has occasionally been possible to spot Snowdon, the highest point of Wales, 224.5km (139½ miles) away.

Descend south of east, with steep drops into Howe of the Caldron on your left. Unless you're in hill fog, once at the plateau edge you'll see Loch Enoch spread below. You'll need to change direction a little, to southeast, down the wide lumpy slope of **Redstone Rig**, aiming just to the right of the islands in Loch Enoch. A small path runs across just above the lochside. Follow this to the right, rising a little as it approaches the southwest corner to avoid steep ground, then descending to the small beach at the southwest corner of **Loch Enoch**.

On the boulder at the exact corner of the loch is a small **memorial**, raised by an Ayrshire walking club, to one T Withers (if I've transcribed him correctly). The plaque has been made by someone with access to a brickworks, by inscribing with a pointed object into an unfired brick.

Descent by Murder Hole

Especially in dry conditions, a descent past Lochs Neldricken and Valley is even more enjoyable than returning via Rig of Loch Enoch and Buchan Hill. The path is rougher than on Rig of Loch Enoch, but it does avoid the rugged descent off Buchan Hill on that route. Distance and time are the same.

A faint and sketchy path continues along the loch shore. Pass below the top end of **Rig of Loch Enoch**, and the tiny col just behind it, and continue to a second tiny col. This is just 300 metres from the loch corner. In the col you'll find the small path, passing to the left of a little pool. ▶ Continue down south, to pass Murder Hole at the corner of **Loch Neldricken**. The path climbs a little

You've now joined Route 6, which has fuller detail of the rest of the walk.

WALKING THE GALLOWAY HILLS

On Rig of Loch Enoch, below Merrick

around the flank of Meaul, and passes alongside **Loch Valley**. It runs beside and then above **Gairland Burn** before slanting down to Loch Trool for the track up to Bruce's Stone and the **car park**.

For Buchan Hill, follow a fence and wall which run up from Loch Enoch's corner in a grassy hollow. At the top of the hollow, head up onto the ridgeline on the left, the **Rig of Loch Enoch**. A small path follows the crest southwest, gently descending, then rising as the Rig of the Buchan to **Buchan Hill**. The first cairn (493m) is the main summit. The summit ridge bends right, southwest, to a final cairn.

Slant down southwest. The upper slope of Buchan Hill has low crags called **Black Gairy**. The southwest direction from the summit will bring you into a wide, grassy gap, with a rough path continuing below. (If, having ignored the compass, you do arrive above low crags, a bit of casting around will reveal a way down between them.)

If the stream is in spate, head straight downhill towards Buchan house, to rejoin the track there and head up right to the car park.

Continue slanting southwest, towards **Buchan Burn**. After some very rough ground near the burn, you can cross the burn to the well-used path on the western bank, leading down to the **car park**. ◄

ROUTE 6
The Three Lochs

Start/finish	Bruce's Stone, upper car park (NX 415 804)
Distance	11.5km (7½ miles)
Ascent	550m (1800ft)
Harshness	3
Approx time	4hr
Terrain	Coarse grassland ascent is followed by easier ground and rocky slabs; then small paths, becoming rough on descent
Highest point	Rig of Loch Enoch, 545m
Parking	Two car parks at Bruce's Stone: the route starts from the higher one at the road's end
Variants	At Loch Enoch, wild Galloway is all around you. Continue to Merrick (reversing Route 5, or via the Caldron, Route 10), or to Craignaw (reversing Route 7). Or make the rough circuit of Loch Enoch, perhaps including Mullwharchar.

Open out the Galloway map and the place is an accident in a blue-paint factory. For its size, this area is more lake-infested even than England's well-known Lake District. Starting at Loch Trool, this walk passes through the heart of the rough country to the highest, most central and must crucial loch of them all: Loch Enoch.

Loch Enoch sprawls like an amoeba across a square kilometre of granite bedrock. Its little beaches are silver granite sand. That sand is pure quartz, the crystals still sharp, so that it was once gathered to make into whetstones for scythes. The loch itself is bottomless, it never freezes over, and the largest of its islands itself contains a small peat pool, the Loch in the Loch. The first of those statements is unlikely and the second one is untrue: I have crossed the ice of Loch Enoch to visit that island with its lochan, and so has someone I met at Merrick summit while researching this book. People have also swum Loch Enoch to the island. The Loch in the Loch is reported as pleasantly warm on a summer's day, but the swim back will quickly cool you down again. (Note that these crossings are not being recommended to readers of this book: both the swim and the ice-walk have obvious dangers.)

The start of the walk is rough, especially in high summer. But tussock times are forgotten as you reach the gentle, grippy hornfels slabs on the upper part of Buchan Hill. The route continues along a low-altitude ridgeline with a small path, to the sudden arrival at Loch Enoch, and returns past two more lovely, lonely lochs – for a short outing that encapsulates all of what Galloway is good at.

From the top end of the upper car park, the wide Merrick path with noticeboard at its foot slants uphill among scattered trees. Through a small decomposed gate it arrives above the **Buchan Burn**. Where the path runs alongside the burn, cross it and pass through a broken wall.

Winter alternative
In normal summer conditions the Buchan Burn can easily be crossed, and often in winter as well. If the burn is full, the alternative route is to descend the track from the top of the car park, down a steep zigzag and then across

Loch Enoch and Mullwharchar

ROUTE 6 – THE THREE LOCHS

a stone bridge over Buchan Burn. At once, head up a sketchy path alongside the burn, with very tough vegetation cover in high summer, but some waterfalls to enjoy.

Head up to the right of the burn in very rough grassland. (It gets a little better higher up.) Head roughly northeast, up the crest of a poorly defined moorland spur where the vegetation is somewhat less luxuriant. ▶ Ahead, the broken crags of **Black Gairy** cross the upper slope of Buchan Hill. While a way can be made up through these, the better route is to head to the left of them, to a small level shoulder at 340m altitude. ▶ Cross the level plateau to a clump of strangely stripy rocks (NX 4206 8143). Here, you confront the rather steeper but actually very friendly rocks of Buchan Hill's west face.

A grassy groove slants up to the right through the lower rocks. Above that, head directly uphill. Many gently angled slabs of bare rock, in rough and broken hornfels, help you romp uphill to the cairn at the southwest corner of **Buchan Hill**.

The trace of a path leads northeast to another cairn, then north to the third. It then runs downhill for the start

Suckler cows graze here – see Route 8.

A different line, easier to navigate, is recommended if descending: see Route 5.

Lunch stop above Loch Neldricken on Rig of the Buchan

of Rig of the Buchan. In due course this becomes the **Rig of Loch Enoch**. At the base of the final rise, a path contours out left to meet a fence in the hollow down to the left of the ridgeline. ◄ Cross the fence ahead and head up left for 100 metres or so for the little cliff holding the Grey Man of the Merrick (NX 436 845). Then follow the hollow up to the col at its top. Turn up to the right to arrive suddenly at a rock-and-grass headland directly above the southwest corner of **Loch Enoch**.

> Or keep north up the ridgeline, missing out on the Grey Man in favour of an even more dramatic arrival at Enoch.

The **Grey Man of the Merrick** is a small rock face which, seen sideways on, resembles a rather craggy sort of human face. You need to look from uphill to see the effect. A few years back, this bit of rock face fell away; but, by a happy chance, the remaining rocks (Son of Grey Man) once again resemble a face.

Above Loch Enoch, turn right, with a trace of path, to a col just above the loch at the top of a tiny valley running down to the right. (This is the Gutter; if taken by mistake, it gives a quick but wet way down to Loch Valley, sloping above the Murder Hole and to the west of Meaul hump.) Keep up ahead, to cross over the next hump and drop to the head of a second tiny valley running down to

ROUTE 6 – THE THREE LOCHS

the right. From the col just above the loch, a small path passes to the left of a tiny pool and runs on down the little valley. The small and little-visited **Loch Arron** is seen over to the left of the path.

Loch Arron is the haunt of the **peat bog hags** who appear in the form of naked maidens smeared with black mud. This startling sight is disconcerting to some hillwalkers. These blackened lassies haven't been sighted in the flesh since the permissive mid 1970s, although their legend lives on in south Ayrshire.

The path runs down to the western corner of **Loch Neldricken**, where a reedy hollow next to the shore is the fabled Murder Hole.

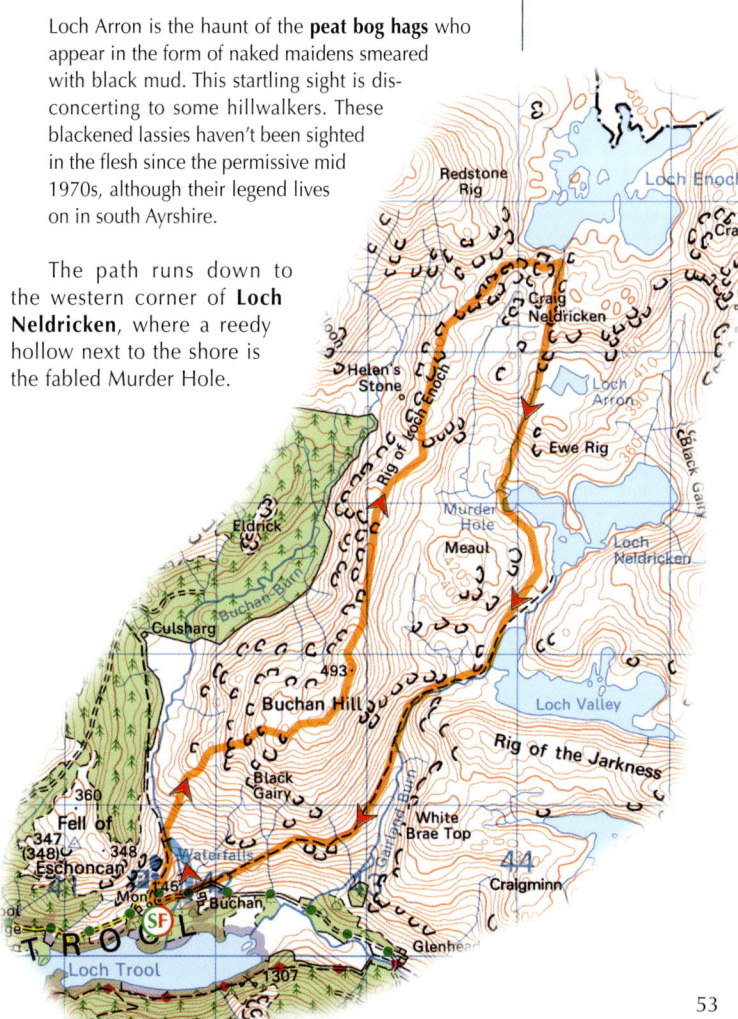

The path bends briefly around the shoreline then rises gently southeast to round the shoulder of the hump Meaul and descend to the western end of **Loch Valley**. Paths run above the loch then join together to run down to the right of the outflow stream, Gairland Burn, in a V-form hanging valley.

THE MURDER HOLE

Like Doone Valley on Exmoor, the Murder Hole is a fictional place that's managed to get itself marked on real maps:

> The unplumbed depths of the Murder Hole. It never froze; it was never whitened with snow. With open mouth it lay ever waiting like an insatiable beast for its tribute of human life; it never gave up a body committed to its depths, or broke a murderer's trust.

It's in SR Crockett's *The Raiders* that the fierce tribes of Macaterick and Faa strip hillwalker victims of our expensive Gore-Tex and electronics and dump us in this convenient corner of the loch.

After 800 metres, the bog-and-boulder path contours forward as the stream drops away. It rounds the slope of **Buchan Hill** and threads behind a small knoll, to a sudden view onto Loch Trool. The path has a broken wall immediately below it, running down to a former gate. The path slants on downhill, tangled in deep bracken during July and August, to join a track in woods at the slope foot.

The track crosses an old bridge over Buchan Burn and rises steeply (known as the 'Killer Brae'). As it bends sharply right, keep ahead up a rocky little path to the Bruce's Stone (**Mon** on the map) above Loch Trool. ◄ Take either of the broad paths to the right to reach the upper **car park**, or a small path down ahead in trees for the lower one.

For battle detail, see Route 3 or the info boards on site.

ROUTE 7

Craignaw

Start/finish	Bruce's Stone, upper car park (NX 415 804)
Distance	15.5km (9½ miles)
Ascent	750m (2500ft)
Harshness	4
Approx time	6hr 30min
Terrain	Rough paths, tough vegetation alongside Loch Neldricken and above Buchan Burn, slabby granite on Craignaw
Highest point	Craignaw, 645m
Parking	Two car parks at Bruce's Stone: the route starts from the higher one at the road's end
Variants	You can include Dungeon Hill (which is also in Route 16). This adds 1km (about 20min) to the walk but you miss a nice bit of granite ground above Wolf Slock.

If you're reading through this book in order, you're thinking that I'm one of those authors who hypes up every single route as the best there is anywhere. It's not me but the start point at Loch Trool that does this. The easy walk around Loch Trool, the high route over the Merrick, the expedition to Loch Enoch: these introduce the best that the Galloway Highlands have to offer. Specifically, they introduce Craignaw – which, in Galloway terms, is the hill that has it.

Don't be misled by the way Craignaw is 198m lower than Merrick. Craignaw is the one that rises in bare, glacier-scraped granite. Craignaw is the one where the goats go, where the tussocks are green and grim, where the Devil plays at bowls with erratic boulders on a lawn that's bare rock. Rising out of the grass and peat, those grey slabs make great, easy walking; and from Point of the Snibe in the south over to the Brishie ridge, one step in two on this hill will be on that naked granite.

Climb just Craignaw, and this book will have earned its cover price. But after these first few routes, you'll have acquired the Galloway habit, ready to seek out the less accessible delights of Curleywee, Hoodens Hill and the northern approach to Cairnsmore of Fleet. Happy Galloway!

Walking the Galloway Hills

From the upper car park, take a gravel path to Bruce's Stone (**Mon** on the map) overlooking Loch Trool. ◀ Turn left down a small path where the peat is eroded down to bare rock. It joins a track descending from the upper car park to cross a bridge over **Buchan Burn**. In another 250 metres, take a field gate on the left, with a signboard for Loch Valley, for the start of a rough path.

From the lower, dual-carriageway car park, there's a small path up to the right of the road to Bruce's Stone.

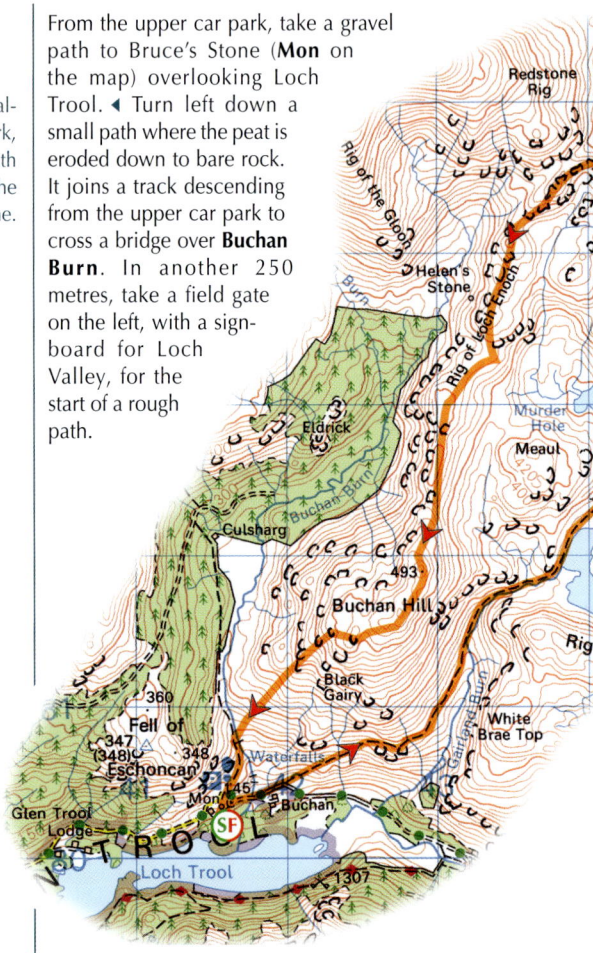

The path curves round into the valley of the **Gairland Burn**. It runs up to the left of the burn to arrive at the outflow of **Loch Valley**. It passes to the left of Loch Valley, rather soft and wet. The path here is divided,

ROUTE 7 – CRAIGNAW

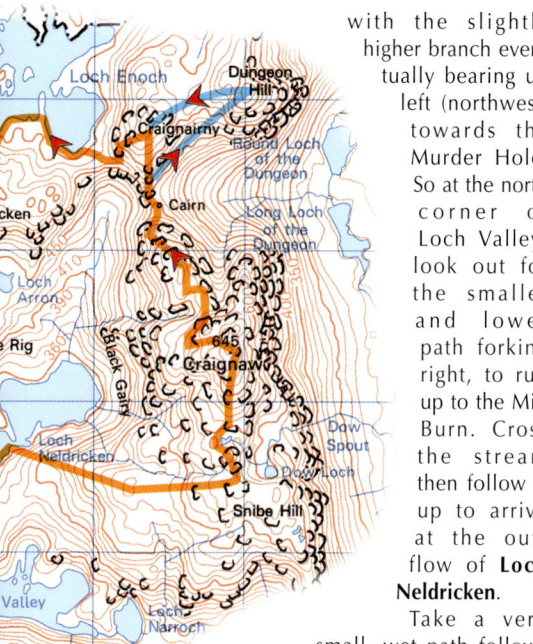

with the slightly higher branch eventually bearing up left (northwest) towards the Murder Hole. So at the north corner of Loch Valley, look out for the smaller and lower path forking right, to run up to the Mid Burn. Cross the stream then follow it up to arrive at the outflow of **Loch Neldricken**.

Take a very small, wet path following the loch's southern shore. After 500 metres, opposite a long promontory from the northern shore, turn uphill. Follow a broad spurline up east onto the ridge of **Craignaw**. Along the broad crest the going is rather good, with slabs of bare granite leading up to the summit cairn.

The way off Craignaw is a little awkward, even in clear weather. The best way down is to head just north of west for 400 metres, descending rocky but not steep ground to a level shoulder. Now contour to the right, with a slight rise onto a flat-topped spur. Here is the boulder-sprinkled slab called the Devil's Bowling Green. Follow the spur's flat top northwest, until a small path leads north down off its end to a col with a tall cairn (named Nick of the Dungeon on Harvey maps). ▸ At the col's cairn, the faint path divides.

The rock-fringed hollow down left, unnamed on maps, is the Wolf Slock.

Diversion to Dungeon

For Dungeon Hill, take the path slanting up to the right, northeast. After 800 metres, it fades away on the complicated knolly plateau of Dungeon Hill. Keep ahead, to the plateau's eastern corner, to find the cairned high point of **Dungeon Hill**, which is distinguished as Scotland's lowest 2000-footer summit.

Return west across the lumpy plateau, along the top of steep ground dropping to the left, to find the cairn on the granite knob of **Craignairny**.

If you don't want to visit Dungeon Hill, just keep straight ahead up to Craignairny. This is delightful. After granite slabs forming the tops of drops to the left, the ridge rises in little rocky steps, which you can scramble up or zigzag around to reach the small cairn on **Craignairny**, a very fine viewpoint above Loch Enoch.

Make a way down slabby ground to the saddle leading towards Craig Neldricken. Then drop right, through coarse grasses, to the southeast corner of **Loch Enoch** just below. Follow a small, rough path heading west above the loch shore, crossing the base of a long, thin promontory. (Don't shortcut across ground up left; that way, bogs lie.) Just 300 metres short of the loch's southwest corner, a tiny col is just up to the left: this is the start of an alternative descent by the Murder Hole (see Route 6). Continue past a second tiny col onto the rise behind it, which stands immediately above the loch's southwest corner. ◄

> It's tempting to continue ahead up Merrick. Yield to this urge by all means; but for an easier ascent, head north above the loch for 300 metres before turning uphill.

South ridge of Craignairny above Wolf Slock

ROUTE 7 – CRAIGNAW

This is the top end of the **Rig of Loch Enoch**. A small path follows the crest of this low ridgeline southwest, all the way to **Buchan Hill** – the first cairn is the main summit. The summit ridge bends right, southwest, to a final cairn.

The upper slope of Buchan Hill has low crags called **Black Gairy**. Continuing down southwest will bring you into a wide, grassy gap, with a rough path continuing below. Keep slanting southwest, towards **Buchan Burn**. After some very rough ground near the burn, you can cross the burn to a well-used path on the western bank, and this leads down to the **car park**. ▶

Devil's Bowling Green, Craignaw

If the stream is in spate, head straight downhill towards Buchan house. Rejoin the track there and head up right to the car park.

WALKING THE GALLOWAY HILLS

ROUTE 8
Craiglee and Rig of the Jarkness

Start/finish	Bruce's Stone, upper car park (NX 415 804)
Distance	13.5km (8½ miles)
Ascent	550m (1800ft)
Harshness	5
Approx time	5hr
Terrain	Tough ground of grass and granite, with some little scrambly crags (optional)
Highest point	Craiglee, 531m
Parking	Two car parks at Bruce's Stone: the route starts from the higher one at the road's end
Variants	You can tack this one onto the end of Route 9 for an outing that's tough and also rather long – see Route 9 for details

In Galloway, the lower slopes are harsh, the tops smooth and gentle. But Craiglee of Dee, at only 531m, consists entirely of 'lower slopes'. In summer, the ridgeline is calf-deep in coarse, ebullient grasses, with a few black peaty paths trampled by the cattle.

But for tough trampers of the two-legged kind, Craiglee offers many rewards. This is a granite hill, with a fine trig point mounted on bare rock, and some scrambly little crags available on the way up. The Rig of the Jarkness is every bit as good as its name, speckled with boulders, spotted with lochans, and with water to look down on on both sides. And if you love this Craiglee, you may also like Craiglee of Doon (Route 15).

Take a wide path from the upper car park to Bruce's Stone (**Mon** on the map), high above Loch Trool. ◄ To the left of the stone, a small, rather rocky path descends to join a track just below. Keep ahead down this, across Buchan Burn on a stone bridge and through ancient oakwoods. After crossing **Gairland Burn** on a wooden bridge, keep right where a track to Glenhead turns off left, and cross **Glenhead Burn** on an ugly modern bridge.

If you have parked at the lower car park, follow a very narrow path to the right of the road up to Bruce's Stone.

ROUTE 8 – CRAIGLEE AND RIG OF THE JARKNESS

The track (now signed as the Southern Upland Way) slants uphill in a plantation to join a wide, smooth track. Turn left on this, gently uphill and soon on open hillside. After 3km, as the track levels off before descending towards Loch Dee, take a wide gate through a fence on your left.

Head northeast through very rough, peaty grassland, to gain the base of Craiglee's gentle southwest ridgeline. This features little slantwise granite cliffs, and you can make much of the going along the slabby tops of these. There's even a faint path along the final ridge to the rock-mounted trig point of **Craiglee**.

Around 2010, the farmer here abandoned arduous and unprofitable sheep, and substituted a herd of mixed-breed **suckler cows**. They include some of the distinctive black-with-white-stripe Belted Galloways. The cattle supposedly improve the hillside, but in fact trample the peaty ground to bits, making the going on Craiglee even rougher than it was before.

Granite scrambling on the southwest spur of Craiglee

The cattle are wild and rather boisterous. If they approach closer than you care for, flapping a map at them should scare them away. They should not pose any danger unless you pass between a cow and her young calf – which shouldn't happen, as they're not supposed to be calving up here. If you have a dog, prepare to let it off the lead if cows become hostile to it.

Head north over a mix of bare rock and reasonable grassland (cow-trampled in places) for about 250 metres, then bend northwest, descending onto the wide ridgeline Rig of the Jarkness. You'll pass at least one small pool,

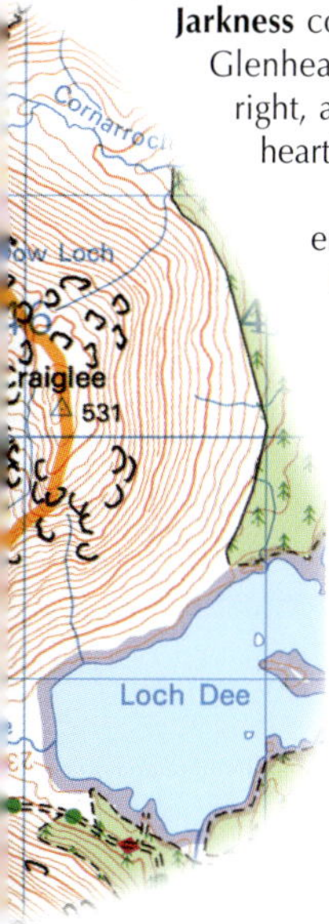

Loch Dee and Craiglee

then keep to left of the 200-metre-long **Dow Loch**. In mist, only a careful compass bearing will let you find it among the small crags – but it doesn't really matter if you don't find it. The bumpy ridgeline of **Rig of the Jarkness** continues west-northwest, with the two Glenhead Lochs down left, Loch Valley down right, and magnificent views across the rough heartland to Merrick.

After passing Loch Valley, at its very end the ridgeline steepens towards crag. Descend to a little level plateau, then turn down right, northeast, to cross **Gairland Burn** to the rough path beyond it. Turn down left. ▶ The path runs down to the right of the burn through a V-shaped slot valley, then eases round to the right to a sudden view down to Loch Trool; the foot of the path has, in high summer, some fearsome bracken.

A rougher path to left of the burn gives better views of the tumbling waterfalls.

Rejoin the outward track and turn right, either revisiting Bruce's Stone or following the track all the way up to the **car parks**.

ROUTE 9
Mulldonoch to Curleywee

Start/finish	Bruce's Stone, lower car park (NX 414 802)
Distance	19.5km (12 miles)
Ascent	950m (3200ft)
Harshness	4
Approx time	7hr 30min
Terrain	Rough grassland with optional scrambly outcrops; grassy ridges with small path; short stretch of deep vegetation to reach path above White Laggan, then tracks to finish
Highest point	Lamachan Hill, 717m
Parking	Two car parks at Bruce's Stone: the route starts from the lower one
Variants	If you found this route comfortable and are up for a slightly tougher add-on, then after Loch Dee switch into Route 8. The combined route is 23.5km (14½ miles) with 1200m (4000ft) ascent – about 9hr.

This route is classic Galloway: an ascent over rough grass with plenty of little outcrops for scrambling on is complemented by the easier walking along the high ridgeline. Also typically Galloway is the 200-metre stretch of really rough grassland to reach the path above White Laggan.

Mulldonoch is a tricky hill to get onto. Approaches from Loch Trool involve plantations, very steep rough ground, and a deer fence along the top of recent broadleaf plantations. (In about 2035 there may be an attractive approach above Pulharrow Burn through these future trees.) The devious route offered here is by far the most comfortable. Even so, the ancient forest track is on the point of vanishing into the undergrowth. Its marking on the 2019 Harvey map, and in this guidebook, should be enough to keep it open. Walkers who are public spirited enough to bring up some secateurs could snip back one or two of the encroaching branches or brambles.

Curleywee, the climax of this route, is one of the two Galloway hills that aficionados may consider as even better than the Merrick (the other being Craignaw, Route 7). As with Mulldonoch, its approaches are awkward, the descent given here being the most comfortable.

Route 9 – Mulldonoch to Curleywee

From the lower, dual-carriageway car park, head up the road for a few steps to cross a culvert. Take a path on the right leading up under trees to Bruce's Stone (**Mon** on the map), high above Loch Trool.

Keep ahead down a small, steep path eroded to bare hornfels rock. ▶ The path joins a track, continuing downhill then over a stone bridge with a waterfall upstream, to run through oakwoods. After another bridge, over **Gairland Burn**, ignore a track forking left and marked 'dominus fecit' – leading to something the Good Lord himself didn't directly *fecit* (construct), a chalet hut settlement. The main track crosses **Glenhead Burn** and climbs in plantations to join a bigger track.

> The granite contact is only a couple of hundred metres away; the Bruce's Stone is a granite erratic found in situ.

Turn left for 600 metres. Immediately before the track crosses the **Sheil Burn** (with waterfalls on the high slope above), it's time to start seeking out the overgrown old track that's the key to Mulldonoch. Turn up right, on a faint path on the stony footing of the vanished track. It slants up right (southwest) for a few steps, then does a brief zigzag left and back right. It continues northwest, slanting gently uphill and then contouring.

After 400 metres from leaving the track, the path slants uphill again, roughly west. It crosses one tiny stream to a culvert over a second stream. Immediately before this stream (NX 4297 7938), the vanished track forks. Turn uphill, soon slanting left away from the stream, then back right to approach another stream. Here, the path turns directly uphill through a tree gap, with small self-sown trees threatening to encroach. ▶

> If carrying secateurs, please deploy them here.

Emerging at the top of plantations, you are above the bad vegetation zones, and can make any way you fancy up Mulldonoch. The following complicated route is a very nice one, but improvising could be even more enjoyable – or possibly not, if your route choice is unlucky.

The faint path continues uphill, with the little stream nearby on the right. After 300 metres you reach a slight shelf, and bend right to contour above the stream top and behind a tiny hump called Gawintoms. The path descends a little, to cross a grassy hollow. Here, the path fades away; but head to a cairn perched on a boulder ahead and slightly uphill (NX 4250 7914).

Head directly uphill, taking advantage of all the gentle rocky outcrops or the lower vegetation alongside them. After 300 metres, contour across the top of the grassy hollow on your right to the level spur beyond. The spur has a granite boulder that isn't a true rocking stone but can be persuaded to jiggle. And its tip is an outstanding viewpoint above Loch Trool.

Here and there on the Galloway Hills, there used to be **rocking stones**, granite boulders, carefully deposited by melting ice, that would sway when vigorously pushed. Back in the

On the north slope of Mulldonoch

1970s, I quite often came across them. However, humans always want to find out how far things will go, and in the case of a rocking stone the answer is: far enough to fall off its support and cease to be a rocking stone. Any still remaining will be ones unmarked on maps or hidden deep in plantations.

Return along the spur, with a small path. This bends left, east, to the foot of a sequence of rocky outcrops. Head up among, or over, these, to reach the cairned northwest summit, and past a pool to the main summit of **Mulldonoch** just beyond.

Head south across a wide saddle with pools, and up the fairly steep slope of **Cambrick Hill**. Gentle grassy walking leads to the wide, flat summit of **Lamachan Hill**, with a shelter cairn at the top of a broken wall near the southern rim.

Turn back sharp left, northeast, and follow a line of old iron fence posts to the rugged little side top **Bennanbrack**. ◀ Head down the bumpy ridgeline southeast towards the fine cone of Curleywee ahead. After 400 metres, you come to a small col, and it's worth seeking out the small goat path which slants out left here, to run along the top of the steep north-facing slope. But if it's missed, the ridge crest is almost as nice. Either path leads down to the wide saddle Nick of Curleywee. A broken wall runs across the saddle; pass through a gap in the wall, and head up onto Curleywee.

Bennanbrack is from Binnein Breac, the speckled peak.

The 'country rock' of the Southern Uplands is ocean-floor sludges. It comes in two different forms, which are displayed side by side at the foot of **Curleywee**'s cone in a two-coloured outcrop, divided pale and dark grey (NX 4513 7686).

Curleywee seen from Bennanbrack

ROUTE 9 – MULLDONOCH TO CURLEYWEE

The paler rock is the standard greywacke, a massive and solid bed formed from a single underwater mudslide. The darker, layered Moffat Shale was a steady trickle of finer silt, probably coming down from a different direction off a different part of the continental shelf. Sharp-eyed, lucky observers might spot a graptolite fossil, a little scratchy mark a few centimetres long, in the shaly screes.

Continue uphill, keeping to the right of patches of shaly scree, then among shaly outcrops, to the satisfying summit of **Curleywee**. Descend gently southeast to the shoulder called Gaharn. ▶ Now descend a grassy spurline northeast. As it steepens, turn down directly east, seeking out the slightly higher lines rather than the grassy hollows. At the slope foot, keeping well to left of a fenceline, cross seriously tussocky ground to reach a path.

> Descent north over White Hill leads to a very steep, albeit grassy, descent to the forest track below.

The path, which has a few soggy bits, leads down north through plantations to arrive above **White Laggan bothy**. After crossing a stream, drop to the bothy, for a wide path leading down to a wide, smooth track. Turn left, passing above **Loch Dee** and rising to a watershed pass.

On the right, you pass the **Axe Head Stone**, one of the seven sculptural stones decorating the 7stanes mountain biking areas. It celebrates the way the giants of Scotland and Ireland used to throw things like this at each other across St George's Channel. The runes are an ancient Irish poem, *The Mystery*, by Amergin: 'I am the ox of the seven combats / I am the vulture upon the rocks / I am a beam of the sun'.

Pass a waymark post on your left and continue down the track. ▶ The track runs with **Glenhead Burn** down on its right, to rejoin the outward route. Retrace the outward route back to the **car park**.

> At the waymark post, you could switch into the extension over Craiglee: see Route 8.

ROUTE 10
Caldron of the Merrick

Start/finish	Bruce's Stone, upper car park (NX 415 804)
Distance	17km (10½ miles)
Ascent	950m (3200ft)
Harshness	5
Approx time	7hr
Terrain	Walk includes rough, pathless ground, steep slopes, and some easy scrambling
Highest point	Merrick, 843m
Parking	Two car parks at Bruce's Stone: the route starts from the higher one at the road's end
Variants	Use the return leg of Route 6 or else Route 7 for an even finer approach

High on the northeast flank of the Merrick lurks a little corrie called the Caldron. Above it lies the airy ridgeline called Little Spear. The enticing names are matched by the actual landscape.

The approach is from Loch Enoch through the heart of rough Galloway. The least arduous way is by the Rig of the Buchan (Route 6). Longer but even better would be to reach Enoch by Loch Neldricken (reversing Route 6) or even Craignaw (Route 7).

A rough hike northwards from Loch Enoch leads to the entry to the Caldron, where a little streamside scrambling is on offer. The slope out of the corrie is challengingly steep, but the Little Spear above is an airy delight. This is a route where the going gets tough – and the tough get a real treat in return for their effort.

Head up the wide Merrick path, then cross **Buchan Burn** down on its right. (This route coincides with Route 6 as far as Loch Enoch; refer to Route 6 for greater detail if needed.) Head up near the stream to a level knoll at 300m level, then up northeast using scrambly rocks onto **Buchan Hill**. Follow the ridgeline north, with a small path, to its sudden arrival just above **Loch Enoch**. ◄

If you want to minimise your appreciation of Loch Enoch, you can now shortcut on a faint path along the loch's west shore.

ROUTE 10 – CALDRON OF THE MERRICK

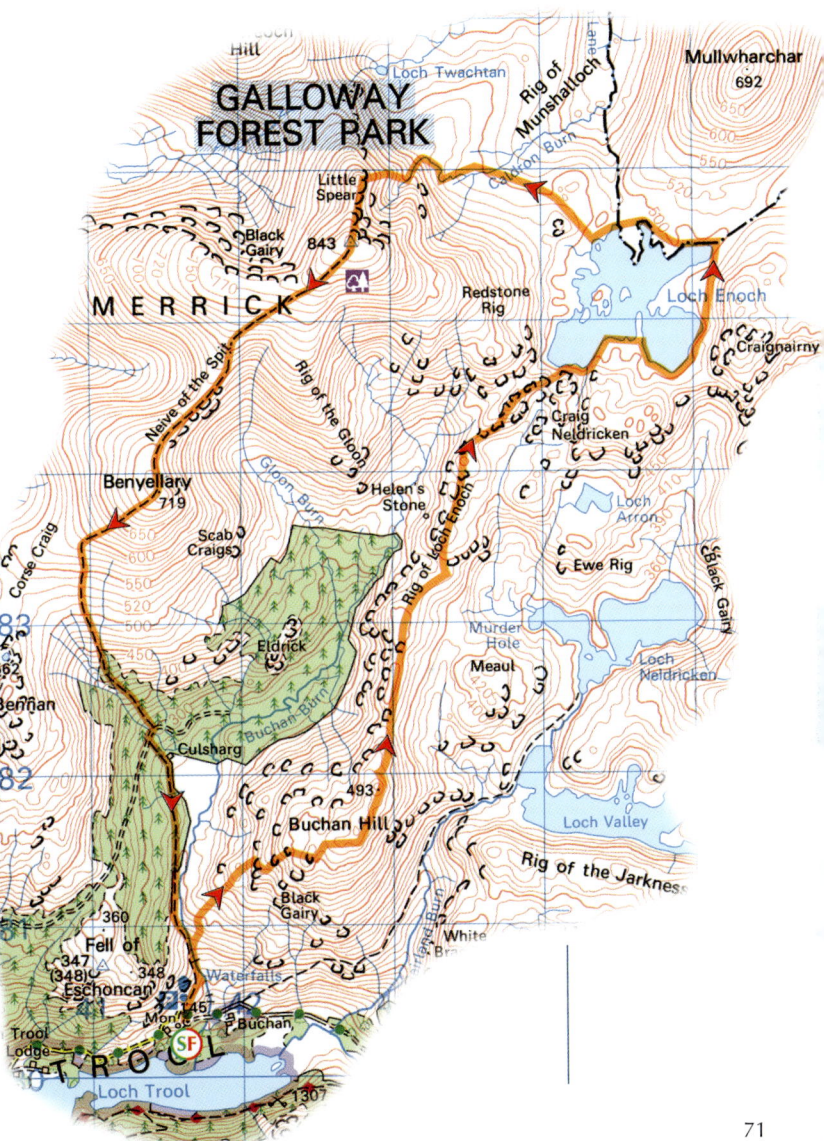

Head east, along (or just above) Loch Enoch shore, shortcutting across a thin promontory, to the beach at the loch's southeast corner. A faint path now runs north alongside the shore, aiming towards Mullwharchar over a moorland hump, to reach the beach at Enoch's northeast corner. Traces of path now run along the north shore to the loch's outflow, the Sluice of Loch Enoch.

Cross rugged stepping stones and follow the path southwest along the shore for 250 metres to where a broken fence and wall reach the loch. Follow the fence and wall northwest, staying beside the wall (not the fence) as it veers up left to its high point where **Caldron Burn** emerges from Howe of the Caldron. There's knobbly scrambling to the right of the stream (or heathery slopes alongside) up to a small waterfall and the floor of the corrie hollow.

The bounding ridge to the left of the corrie is a straightforward ascent (steep at the top) to Merrick summit plateau. But more rewarding is the steep spur to the

Little Spear, Kirriereoch Hill and Shalloch, seen from Merrick summit

ROUTE 10 – CALDRON OF THE MERRICK

right of the hollow. As it steepens, rocks projecting from the grass give handholds. You arrive suddenly and satisfyingly at the level top of **Little Spear**. A path runs left along the ridge and up to **Merrick** trig point.

The path leaving the trig point is invisible for its first 20 metres, so take a compass bearing southwest. The path appears and rakes down across a wide, gentle grass slope to a wall corner 200 metres up from the start of **Neive of the Spit** ridgeline. The wall leads along the ridge then up to **Benyellary**.

The heavily used path runs down to left of the wall. Well above the col below, it bends left, south, away from the wall, down to a gate in a deer fence. The rather eroded path runs down through clear-fell then mature plantations.

At a forest road, turn right for a few steps over a stream, then downhill on a good path to pass the austere **Culsharg bothy**. Here, the path turns right and runs through tiny, replanted trees above Buchan Burn to where you left it on the upward walk, with the **car park** just below.

SECTION 2: THE AWFUL HAND

Water of Girvan burn below Cornish Loch, with Shalloch behind (Route 13)

INTRODUCTION

Just how awful is the Awful Hand? It's certainly the biggest and bumpiest of Galloway's three surrounding ridges. Its two ends are two of the area's Corbetts, or 2500-footers; and a metre or two carved out of the col would make Kirriereoch Hill into a third one. However, the name can be divided into two parts. The Awfulness is eastwards, where a high and steep slope drops to the defending bogs that lie to the north of Loch Enoch. The slope is scree and scrappy little rock outcrops, which in really good winters can even be prone to avalanche. Even so, there are grassy parts of it, and the adventurous can find ways if they want to – this book mentions only the northeast face of Merrick (Route 10 in Section 1).

But what makes it a Hand are the five gentle, curving ridges that stretch westwards towards the Water of Minnoch. It's a right-hand hand, the shorter, curved ridge over Benmore being the thumb, with the abandoned cottage of Kirriemore pinched between it and the 'forefinger' ridge of Kirriemore Hill. The fingers aren't Awful at all, but make the natural way to include part or all of the range in horseshoe walks in whatever combination you want. Route 11 combines the middle and forefinger over the two highest hills of the range; the longer Route 12 uses the pinkie finger to Shalloch and the thumb from Benyellary, along the full length of ridge, with access also to the ring finger of Tarfessock. Whatever your combination, the 'Awful' edge eastwards is what you gaze down over to the granite Galloway heartland, as you cross the 'knuckles' of Shalloch, Tarfessock, Kirriereoch, Merrick and Benyellary.

Below the fingertips, the Minnoch valley is planted with conifers. This makes for approaches that are easy going, along the gravel tracks, but also contemplative, with nothing much to see but the trees.

Meanwhile, at the northern end of the range, the high car park at Stinchar Bridge (400m altitude) gives very easy access to Shalloch as the short variant to Route 13. It also gives very tough access to some low and lumpy summits of a different sort, the gnarled and outcropped Craigmasheenie and Shiel Hill, with the heather-embedded pools of Cornish Loch and Loch Girvan Eye. In a rare act of compassion, Forestry and Land Scotland have created a swamp-free and gravelled path to the first of these two (see Route 14).

ROUTE 11
Kirriereoch Hill and Merrick

Start/finish	Kirriereoch farm track (NX 358 866)
Distance	19km (12 miles)
Ascent	900m (3000ft)
Harshness	3
Approx time	6hr 30min
Terrain	Forest roads, two short sections of forest rides; ridges of mostly short grass
Highest point	Merrick, 843m
Parking	Picnic place just east of Water of Minnoch; smooth forest track, signed for parking from the Straiton road
Variants	Recommended: finish over Benyellary (as Route 12) is 20km (12½ miles) with 900m (3000ft) ascent – about 7hr

This alternative route up Merrick does involve several miles of forest plodding, and a very small amount of swampy forest ride. The reward is the back way up Merrick that's even better than the busy Neive of the Spit route from Loch Trool (Route 5) – as well as being very much quieter. Once above the forest, the crossing of Kirriereoch Hill is on delightful smooth grass, with great views of Merrick's exciting side. And that exciting side, up the Little Spear and the airy little northern ridgeline, is the connoisseur's way up this hill. The impressionable might even consider it as the Southern Upland equivalent of Ben Nevis's better way by the Carn Mor Dearg Arête.

If you take the longer descent by Benyellary, you get that fine Neive of the Spit anyway. Even better would be a wilder descent to Loch Enoch – but that would require some transport to pick you up at Loch Trool.

Head east along the smooth gravel track. Where it bends left, an older track on the right loops out to a gateway for a view across Kirriereoch Loch towards Merrick. With **Kirriereoch farm** just ahead, the main track bends right again, generally northeast, passing side tracks on the right (return route) and left (for Tarfessock farm).

ROUTE 11 – KIRRIEREOCH HILL AND MERRICK

In another 1.3km, the track crosses **Pillow Burn**. (Note the smallness of this burn: it ought to be draining the corrie between Tarfessock and Kirriereoch Hill, but isn't!) The track then bends right (east) to a junction. ▶ Keep ahead here for 800 metres. The track descends slightly, bending to the left, then ascends briefly to a small grassy lay-by on the right (the track crosses a small stream just ahead). On the right immediately behind the lay-by is a small knoll of grassed-over rock. Head south past this knoll and across the small stream into a tree gap. Follow this down to reach open ground at the head of Pillow Burn.

With a decayed fence ahead, turn left along the foot of the plantations, negotiating the small swamp at the foot of the tree gap. Cross the substantial **Cross Burn** to the foot of Kirriereoch's west ridgeline.

Left would be for Shalloch on Minnoch, Route 12.

> The **Cross Burn** descending from Balminnoch corrie perversely carries its waters southwards, away from its natural flow line along Pillow Burn, to deposit them in the Kirriemore Burn instead. This probably dates from the end of the Ice Age, with a lump of leftover glacier diverting the stream along its edge. By the time the last ice melted, the diverted stream line had eroded down far enough to become permanent.

Little Spear ridge to Merrick

WALKING THE GALLOWAY HILLS

> The Carnirock Stone is quite firmly settled in place and is not a rocking stone – see Route 9.

Cross a decayed stile (NX 3894 8768) onto the foot of the ridgeline. Head uphill, on rapidly improving ground, threading among some scraps of crag. At 564m there's a very minor summit with a small cairn, with the ridge briefly levelling off beyond. Follow some old metal fence posts south; where they bend left (east) is the **Carnirock Stone**, a 3m lump of granite. ◀

CARNIROCK STONE

The stone is made of pale, round-cornered granite. However, when you follow the fence posts uphill for another 50 metres you'll pass a low outcrop of the natural bedrock, which (like the craglets lower down the ridge) is darker, square-cornered greywacke. This shows that the Carnirock and other nearby boulders have been carried here by some glacier.

The low greywacke outcrop provides a further clue. It is a *roche moutonnée*, shaped by the ice; smooth on top but plucked away at its southwest end. This indicates ice flowing over it from the northeast, suggesting that the granite boulders have arrived over the saddle south of Tarfessock, and started their journey on Hoodens Hill. The distinctive granite of Mullwharchar has been carried a lot further than this, reaching to both shores of northern England, and so marking the routes of the spreading ice cap. The visitor centre at Clints of Dromore (Route 31) has a small map of those movements.

Carnirock Stone

A faint path follows the old posts up the gentle grassland. Soon a broken wall arrives from down on the right. At the summit levelling, slant to the right away from the

ROUTE 11 – KIRRIEREOCH HILL AND MERRICK

wall to the tiny summit cairn of **Kirriereoch Hill**. A much larger cairn has been built at a point 100 metres southwest, where there's a natural stonefield to build it from. This offers some shelter and a much better view towards Merrick.

From the true summit of Kirriereoch Hill, descend southeast, to find a wide grass slope down to the saddle in front of Merrick. Descend the left side of the slope; at its foot, go through a broken wall and cross the saddle.

The steep cone of **Little Spear** now rises ahead. Tackle it head-on, to its small unmarked summit above the Caldron corrie. Continue along a short level ridge and up the airy spur to **Merrick** summit with its trig point. For a grand view down onto Loch Enoch, head 250 metres east to the edge of the summit, then retrace your steps to the trig point. ▶

At this point, you may wish to transfer to Route 12 to incorporate Benyellary into a longer but even better route.

If not transferring to Route 12, head down southwest, keeping to the right of the main descent path once it starts to be visible, and instead following the tops of the steep drops on the right. ▶ As a wall arrives from down left, keep between it and the top of the craggy ground of **Black Gairy**. As the ridge ahead starts descending and

In winter these edges can carry cornices.

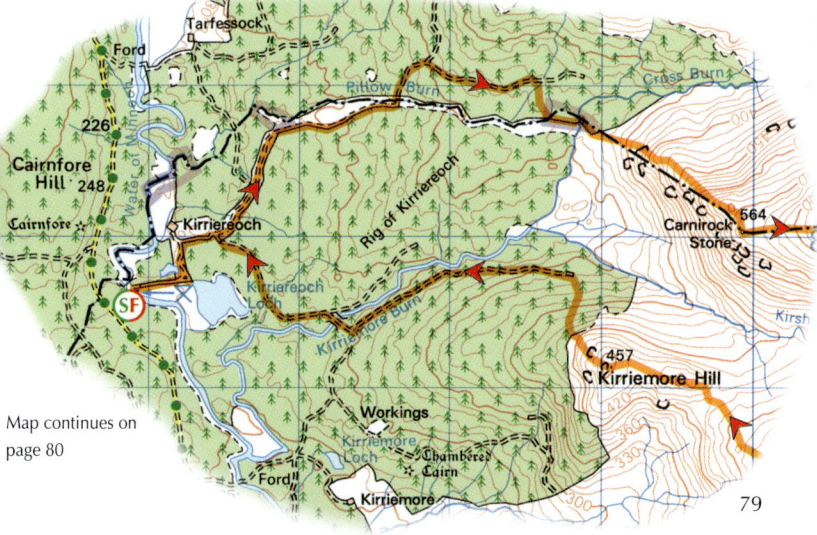

Map continues on page 80

you cross a ruined side wall, pass up to the left of the main wall to follow the ridge crest down westwards.

At 580m, the ridge levels briefly and you pass through another broken wall. Below, the ridge spreads into a wide slope. Head down just north of west, across a wide moorland saddle. In hill fog, those with GPS could aim for a gateway in broken walling at NX 3971 8595, onto the grassier slopes of **Kirriemore Hill**. An upstanding cairn crowns this pleasant wee hill.

Head down northwest, past a knoll with a smaller cairn, to a corner in the forest-top fence. Head left for a few steps, to find a tree-stump-free gap leading down north, with newly planted trees (around 2015) to the left and half-grown ones to the right. It's pathed and grassy, then rough going below, before reaching the corner of a forest track.

Take the lower branch, heading gently down westwards. At a T-junction, turn right across **Kirriemore Burn**. In 300 metres, keep left, to rejoin the outward route near **Kirriereoch farm** and its loch. Retrace the outward route back to the picnic area at the walk start.

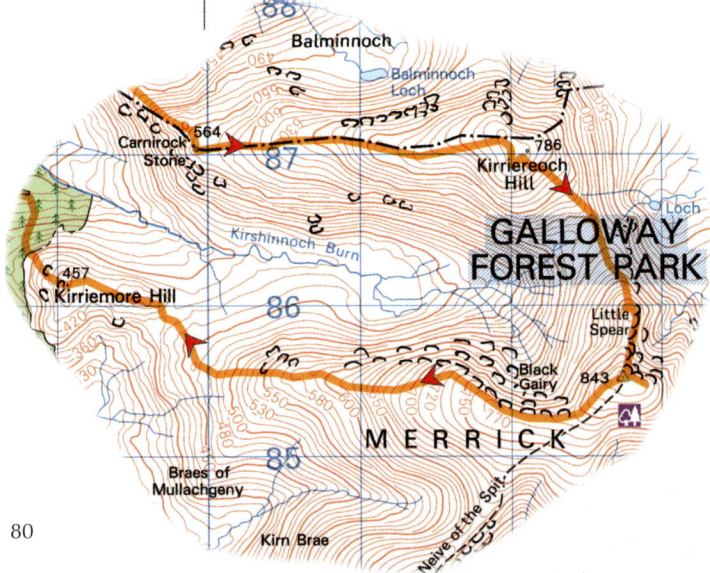

ROUTE 12
The Awful Hand: Shalloch to Benyellary

Start/finish	Kirriereoch farm track (NX 358 866)
Distance	24km (15 miles)
Ascent	1150m (3900ft)
Harshness	4
Approx time	8hr 30min
Terrain	Forest roads, one short section of forest ride; ridges of mostly short grass; steep stony ascent onto Kirriereoch Hill
Highest point	Merrick, 843m
Parking	Picnic place just east of Water of Minnoch; smooth forest track, signed for parking from the Straiton road
Variants	Shorten by leaving out Shalloch: 22km (13½ miles) with 1000m (3400ft) ascent – about 7hr 30min. Can shortcut down off Merrick: see Route 11.

The Awful Hand lives up to its name. Of Galloway's three surrounding ridges, this is the wildest and most challenging. Less walked than the Rhinns of Kells or the Minnigaffs, the going is largely pathless. Rather than a true ridgeline, it's more a linked set of big, separate hills: Shalloch, Kirriereoch and Merrick. The ascent onto Kirriereoch in particular is formidably steep. In hill fog, finding the way down off each hill to the connecting ridge below can be tricky.

The reward for all this is the lovely ground of rocks and pools along Tarfessock; the airy ridgeline of Merrick's Little Spear; and the easier ridgeline of Neive of the Spit at the end of the day.

Head along the forest track eastwards; an older track diverts to the right to a gateway with views across Kirriereoch Loch, then rejoins. The track bends left towards **Kirriereoch farm**, but before reaching it turn right on the main track. Ignore a side track on the right (the return route) and another on the left (towards Tarfessock). The track bends left across **Pillow Burn**, to another fork. ▶ Keep left on the main track.

> The older track to the right is the shorter Route 11 going onto Kirriereoch Hill.

The Awful Hand (Shalloch, Tarfessock, Kirriereoch Hill, Merrick, Benyellary) from the Straiton road

Shortcut to Tarfessock

After 600 metres, a ride (tree gap) on the right has a small stream and an even smaller path. After 300 metres, the ground steepens and the ride becomes unclear (or at least it will be unclear until the early 2020s when young trees will be big enough to see). Keep up due east to exit the plantations at NX 3838 8865. This exit point will be tricky to find if descending this route.

Follow the gentle, grassy ridge up east onto **Tarfessock**.

After passing the ride to Tarfessock, the track forks for a final time. Bear right in a much older track, which ends after 200 metres. Keep ahead, northeast, on what was once a firm, surfaced track but is now a faint, grassy quad-bike trail, to cross **Knocklach Burn**.

The track trace continues up along the forest edge above the stream, then bends up left above the plantation top. Leave it and head up the gentle, grassy ridge to the trig point of **Shalloch on Minnoch**.

Continue just south of east across a slight dip to the small cairn at Shalloch's true summit. Turn downhill, with steep eastward drops (and views) on your left, to find **Nick of Carclach** col. Keep south for the short climb to **Tarfessock**. A cairn with quartz lumps marks the start of the summit plateau; the larger summit cairn is 300 metres beyond.

Alternatively, it looks possible to contour left, across a corrie called Green Holes, to take the gentler northwestern spur – I haven't tried this.

Head down southeast (in mist using care and a compass) to find the continuing ridgeline running bumpily with little pools towards **Kirriereoch Hill**. Cross an old fence to confront the steep slope. ◀ Above the stonefield across its foot (slippery when wet), take advantage of the slight spur at its left edge.

ROUTE 12 – THE AWFUL HAND: SHALLOCH TO BENYELLARY

CLASSIFYING KIRRIEREOCH

The original Harvey map from the 1990s gives the Merrick–Kirriereoch col a spot height of 635m, with Kirriereoch Hill at 786m – a drop of 151m. That would allow Kirriereoch to be designated as a Marilyn (any hill with 150m of drop) but not as a Corbett, which requires 500ft (152m) of drop as well as the 2500ft of altitude that Kirriereoch does satisfy. That would put Kirriereoch in the unique position of a Marilyn that's high enough to be a Corbett but isn't one.

Current OS mapping gives the col a 637m spot height, removing the anomaly. However, that could represent one of the rock knolls rather than the true saddle point!

Before 1981, with no survey of the col other than its contour lines, Kirriereoch was counted as a 'benefit-of-the-doubt' Corbett. It's possible that the next edition of the Harvey map, or the activities of freelance Corbett surveyors, may restore this status. In that case, Route 11, conveniently combining it with the Merrick, will suddenly become somewhat popular.

Cross the plateau, through a fallen wall, to the small summit cairn. (A larger non-summit cairn is 100 metres southwest.) Descend southeast (care in mist) slanting down a wide grass slope, to the next wide saddle. Take the slope of **Little Spear** direct; it's less fearsome than it

The rocky southeast spur of Tarfessock

WALKING THE GALLOWAY HILLS

> To shorten the walk, switch now into Route 11 for a descent from Merrick above Black Gairy.

looks. Cross the narrow, airy summit for the pathed spur up to **Merrick**'s trig point. ◄

The popular Merrick path is not apparent from the trig point. Head southwest to find it becoming clear and peaty as it slants down the grassland called Broads of the Merrick. The grass slope is bounded on the right by a wall. The path joins this wall and follows it downhill to the start of the level **Neive of the Spit** ridge. The path runs to the left of the wall along this ridge for the short rise to **Benyellary**.

Here, the wall bends right, and the path runs quite steeply downhill, still to its left. As the path moves away from the wall, stay with the wall, to the foot of the steeper slope. Here, go through a gateway (NX 4084 8351) and head just north of west down a wide moorland shoulder. The low outcrop of **Corse Craig** is left of the ridgeline route. The going gets rougher, with some heather mixed in with the grasses, as you drop to the wide saddle leading to the perversely named **Benmore** (or Big Hill). Nice, grassier going leads over this to a boulder overlooking Kirkennan Burn and Kirriemore cottage.

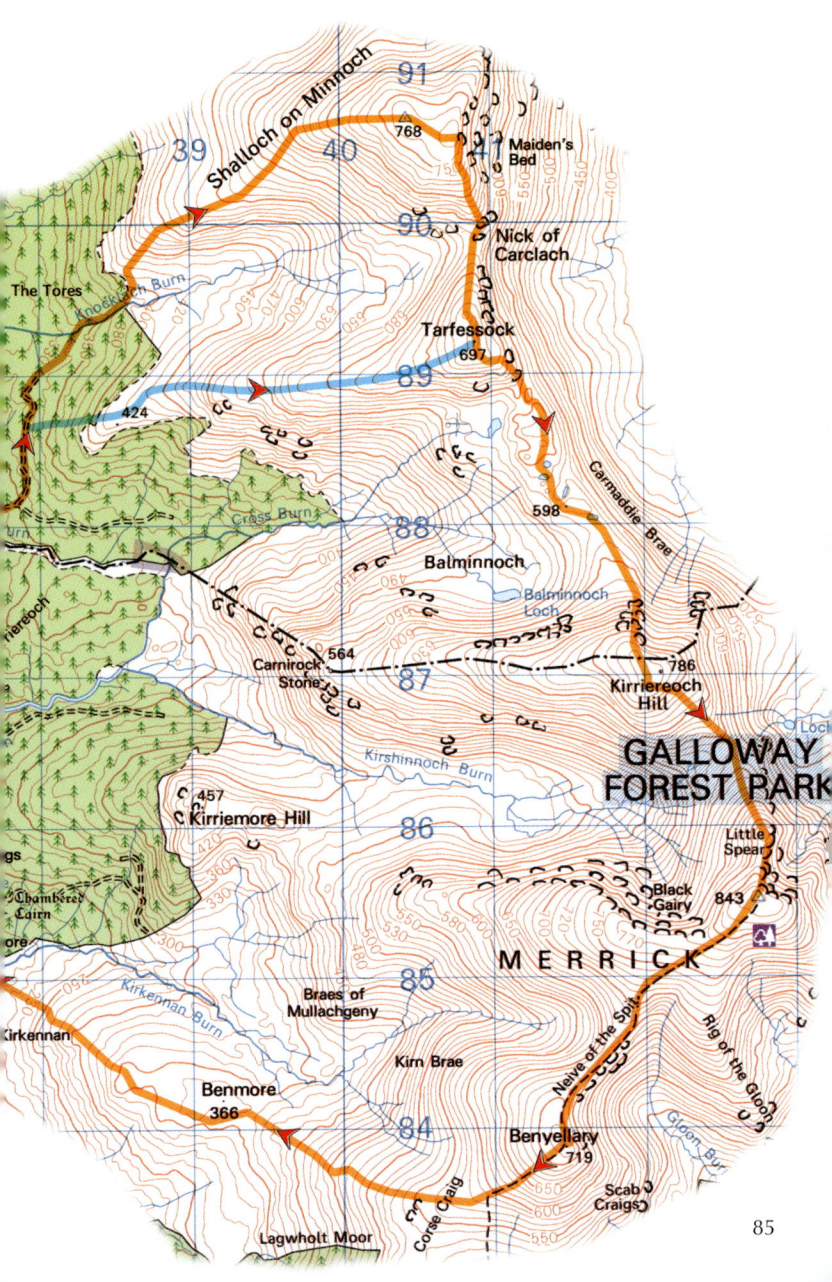

Head straight downhill through broken walls to cross Kirkennan Burn to a gate. Cross a pasture, straight towards the abandoned cottage of **Kirriemore**. Go through a gate and pass round to the left of the cottage to find its very rough access track. This is reinforced with whole tree trunks on its way to meet a forest road. The rough track ahead leads to a ford of Water of Minnoch so turn sharp right, northeast, for 400 metres. At this track junction turn left; in 400 metres, turn left again and cross **Kirriemore Burn**; at the next track junction again keep left. The track passes to the right of **Kirriereoch Loch** to a final junction, where you turn left along the outward route to the picnic spot at Water of Minnoch.

THE AWFUL HAND FROM END TO END

The end-to-end walk of the Awful Hand is a fine ridgewalk over five summits with a high start on the Straiton road and a fine finish at Loch Trool. The difficulty is arranging transport between the two ends. Southwards is the preferred direction. This takes advantage of the Route 13 short version – start from the passing place 1km south of Stinchar Bridge (NX 394 948) and take advantage of the small path over Cairnadloch.

The tough bit is the north slope of Kirriereoch Hill, which is steep and stony. Again, southward travel takes this slope in the easier uphill direction. The full ridge with descent to Bruce's Stone at Loch Trool comes to 16.5km (10½ miles) with 950m (3200ft) of ascent – about 6hr. The reverse direction has 1250m (4200ft) of ascent and takes 45min longer.

ROUTE 13
Shalloch on Minnoch

Start/finish	Stinchar Bridge (NX 396 957)
Distance	14.5km (9 miles)
Ascent	650m (2100ft)
Harshness	4 (or 2 for the straight up-and-down of Shalloch)
Approx time	5hr
Terrain	Rough granite ground for first half, then smooth grassy slopes
Highest point	Shalloch on Minnoch, 775m
Parking	From the minor road, take the tarred side road upstream (forest drive to Loch Doon) and turn left in a track to the unsigned parking area
Variants	Straight up-and-down of Shalloch: 11.5km (7½ miles) with 450m (1500ft) ascent – 3hr 45min

Taken as a straight up-and-down from Stinchar Bridge, Shalloch on Minnoch is a stroll up a grassy slope that makes it the easiest of all the Corbetts (2500-footers) of Scotland – and also, arguably, the least interesting.

Instead, come in by the well-made path over Cornish Hill to take in two of the small but rugged granite summits. Craigmasheenie, in particular, has a harsh charm out of all proportion to its meagre 539m of altitude. Approach Shalloch by its slope edge overlooking the lochs of Galloway's heartland, and save that gentle grassy slope for the descent at the day's end.

Shortcut: straight up Shalloch

From Stinchar Bridge, head south up the minor road. A small parking area is on the right of the road, then a forest track on the left. Just 150 metres after leaving felled plantations, and 800 metres from Stinchar Bridge, a passing place on the left has the start of a small path.

This path leads slightly east of south, crossing a stream, then roughly south up **Cairnadloch** (cairn). The path continues south across level moorland and through

It pains me to transcribe this horrid misspelling of the Gaelic Dubh, meaning black.

a gap in a derelict fence, and up a wide, gentle slope to **Caerloch Dhu**. ◀ The path turns half-left, southeast, along this level shoulder and gently uphill to Shalloch North Top (659m). The path continues south again, across a wide, flat saddle and up a somewhat steeper (but still not steep) slope to the summit plateau of **Shalloch on Minnoch**. There's a trig point and shelter cairn. The true summit is a small cairn 300 metres to the east, and is well worth visiting for its views down into the Galloway heartland.

Return the same way (described in descent at the end of the main route).

From the parking area above **Stinchar Bridge**, cross the side road onto a path signed for Cornish Loch. It crosses River Stinchar by a footbridge. At the junction just beyond, turn left, upstream (now on the path marked on OS maps). The path runs through trees (a memorial just to the right is on the site of one-time Craiglour Lodge), then felled plantation, with neither of the side paths on the left seen on maps being present on the ground. On reaching open moorland, the path, well built and maintained, rises southeast onto **Cornish Hill**. ◀

Don't shortcut now to Craigmasheenie: the slight saving in time is outweighed by the increase in swearwords and soggy feet.

The path doesn't visit the actual summit of the flat-topped hill, but turns down left to **Cornish Loch**. It turns left along the lochside. You can usually cross the outflow without difficulty; if it's in spate, there's a footbridge 200 metres downstream.

From the outflow, head up over rough ground of heather and coarse grasses, which get less harsh as you

Merrick and Shalloch seen from Shiel Hill

rise to the summit of **Shiel Hill** with some poised granite boulders. The trig point, 200 metres north, is perched on bare granite and is worth visiting for its situation and views north.

Return to Shiel Hill summit, and continue on traces of a small path, down southeast then along a level ridgeline south, to the south top above Nick of the Strand. Turn down southwest, on a small path, across the damp little saddle, with the top of sad-looking plantations down to your left. Take the ridge of rocks and rough grasses up **Craigmasheenie**. At the ridge top, which has a small pool, drop right, across a little grass saddle, to Craigmasheenie summit, which is a bare rock.

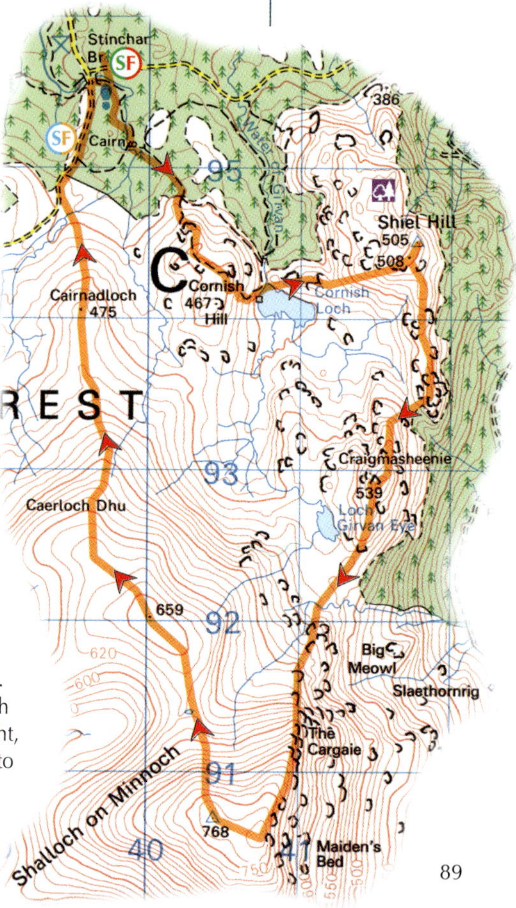

Head down south, on a wide, indefinite ridgeline. Pass well up to the left of **Loch Girvan Eye**. ◀ Rough going follows across level moorland, southwest, through an abandoned fence and across a stream (Craigencoof Burn). You can surmount the first rocky rise, Carglas Craig, or take the grassy valley to its right. Then head up the left edge of the wide slope of Shalloch ahead.

> If visiting the loch, expect rather harsh heather down there.

The going now is pleasantly grassy; or you can move a little to the left to take in the geographical 'featurette' of the **Cargaie**, a vestigial ridgeline forming the left edge of the slope. Either way, arrive on gentler ground alongside a steep drop on the left towards Maiden's Bed. ◀

> In February 2018, this east-facing scarp showed a cornice collapse and major avalanche.

At the highest point of the rim, turn away from the drop to the small summit cairn. Continue just north of west across the plateau for 200 metres to **Shalloch on Minnoch**'s trig point and large shelter cairn.

The descent is fast and easy, although less so if you wander off the small path into the rough moorland. Head north down a mildly steep slope to a saddle where a small path starts. Follow it up the slight rise of Shalloch North Top (659m), and down to the shoulder **Caerloch Dhu**.

Follow the faint path down north, with the ground getting peaty and heathery, across a level saddle where you pass through a gap in a former fence, and then over the slight rise of **Cairnadloch**. The path crosses a stream and reaches the minor road at a passing place just south of the felled plantations. Head north for 800 metres to **Stinchar Bridge**.

STINCHAR FALLS

Maps show a downhill walk through plantations and woodland from Stinchar Bridge to the Stinchar Falls, 4km downstream. These paths have fallen into disuse, and for quite good reason. Although the falls are impressive, they are only partly visible from the airy viewing platform, and very steep slopes mean that the foot of the falls isn't accessible from the erstwhile paths.

The one route to the falls that remains open is the path from Stinchar Bridge starting to the south of the stream to the Aqueduct forest track, then descending from below power lines at NX 380 965.

ROUTE 14
Craigmasheenie and Shiel Hill

Start/finish	Stinchar Bridge (NX 396 957)
Distance	14km (8½ miles)
Ascent	650m (2200ft)
Harshness	5 (short walk: 1)
Approx time	5hr
Terrain	Rough pathless moorland; very rough southwest of Cornish Loch and on the descent off Shiel Hill
Highest point	Craigmasheenie, 539m
Parking	As Route 13
Variants	For a short and much gentler outing, the well-made Cornish Hill walk visits Cornish Hill and Loch: 5.5km (3½ miles) with 150m (500ft) ascent – about 1hr 45min

This is a short but very rugged walk, whose robust vegetation might be best avoided in high summer. The good bits are the wonderfully rocky Craigmasheenie, and the little path line leading to Shiel Hill. The bad bits – you'll find them as you go along.

From the car park entrance, cross the tarmac side road on a wide path to a footbridge over **River Stinchar**. The path continues left through gloomy forest (which will probably be clear-felled in the early 2020s). It recrosses the stream by a much smaller bridge, and reaches open moorland. ▶ The main path zigzags up southwards, passing Megan's Cairn perched on a boulder, and rises to the lumpy plateau of **Cornish Hill**.

For those continuing on the short, well-pathed Cornish Hill walk, a cairn on the right at the start of the plateau can conveniently be considered as Cornish Hill's summit. It has fine views northwards, and the hill's true summit is scarcely worth seeking out. However, those on the full walk are going there anyway.

Two side paths on the left, marked on maps, have been swallowed by undergrowth and are no longer visible on the ground. A spur path right leads to a minor monument.

Cornish Hill short walk

Follow the path as it zigzags down left to **Cornish Loch** and turns left to the loch's outflow. The path continues down to the left of the infant Water of Girvan, soon in plantations. After 200 metres, it crosses the stream by a footbridge. In another 500 metres, the path turns up right, onto the open flanks of **Shiel Hill**. It contours round onto the northwestern spur and heads directly downhill, crossing the end of a forest track, and down through clear-fell to the minor tarmac road.

Turn left, with a bridge over **Water of Girvan**. It's 1km along the road to the car park near **Stinchar Bridge**.

For Craigmasheenie, continue on the good path for about 200 metres, then bear off southwards along the lumpy plateau, with some small swampy pools in the dips. The true top of **Cornish Hill** is a small lump of bare rock.

Descend southeast, keeping well up to the right of **Cornish Loch**. If you meet a fence, don't cross but follow it down left to its corner. Cross a stream (headwater of River Girvan) near the fence corner, and slant up, still southeast, onto the rocky moorland leading towards Craigmasheenie. The going gets gradually a bit less bad.

The final rise is protected by a small swampy pool, with some mini-crags rising behind. Pass to the left of the

Cornish Loch and Shalloch

ROUTE 14 – CRAIGMASHEENIE AND SHIEL HILL

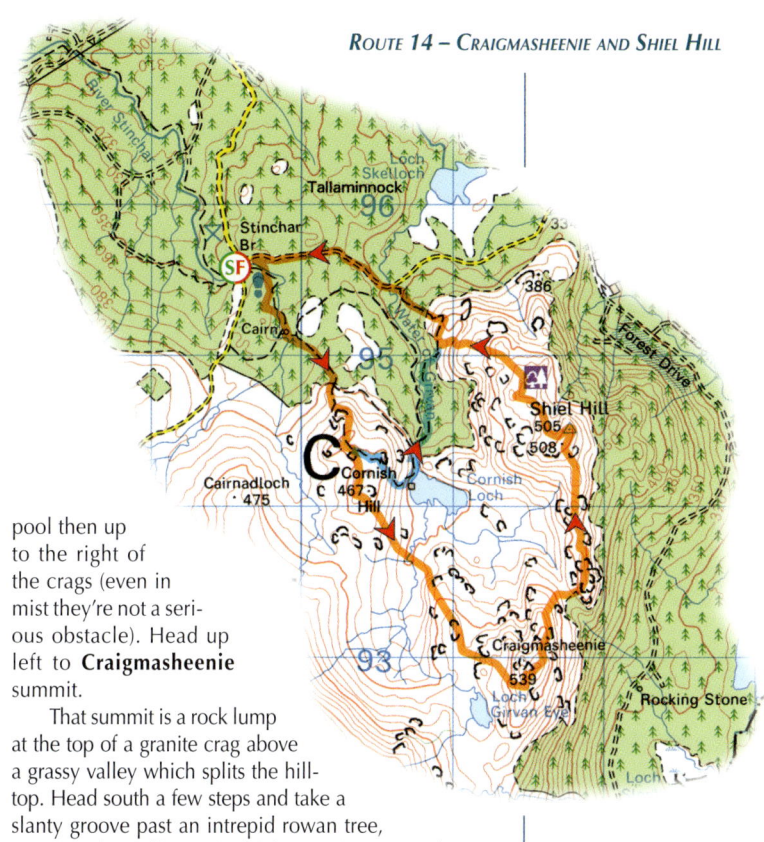

pool then up to the right of the crags (even in mist they're not a serious obstacle). Head up left to **Craigmasheenie** summit.

That summit is a rock lump at the top of a granite crag above a grassy valley which splits the hilltop. Head south a few steps and take a slanty groove past an intrepid rowan tree, crossing the valley at its highest point to reach Craigmasheenie's east top, which has a small pool. Follow the gentle ridge of rocks and grass down northwards to a slight rise and steeper descent behind. Now turn down right, to cross a col (Nick of the Strand) with some brave fir trees clambering into it from down on the right.

A slight rise leads onto the southern ridge-end of Shiel Hill. Follow this north, on comfortable grass, with a faint path. After 400 metres, switch to a parallel ridgeline just to the left. ▶ The faint path leads up to the true top of **Shiel Hill** at 508m, marked by some boulders, and on to the trig point on its granite craglet 200 metres beyond.

The gap has to be a meltwater channel, a former river from the glacier times.

Shiel Hill trig point, looking north into Ayrshire

Return briefly southwest to work around the head of a grassy horseshoe valley, and follow the lumpy moorland a bit west of north. Keep just to the left of the rise of Rowantree Craig, which is the start of a false ridge northwards. Instead of following the false ridge, descend northwest, on worsening ground, to reach a clear path running along the 400m contour.

Follow the path to the right, contouring and then descending northwest to the minor tarmac road. Turn left for 1km along the road to the car park at **Stinchar Bridge**.

CARRICK FOREST DRIVE

Direct access between Stinchar Bridge and the head of Loch Doon is provided by this unsurfaced forest road. It is the usual approach to Tunskeen bothy, and is also the most convenient route from Glentrool Village to Loch Doon (Section 3). It may occasionally be closed off for forest operations. All side tracks are gated off, including the one to Tunskeen.

The 8km of track are well maintained, with a smooth surface; there are loose stones but only occasional potholes. It provides a fine view across Loch Riecawr to Shalloch on Minnoch, and a charming overview of the Carrick Lane stream.

Tickets for the Forest Drive (not expensive) can be purchased, retrospectively if necessary, at the Roundhouse café and osprey observatory near the foot of Loch Doon.

SECTION 3: LOCH DOON

Mullwharchar and Hoodens Hill (Route 16) from Carrick Lane

INTRODUCTION

By this point, while still in the Galloway Highlands, we have entered South Ayrshire – and looking back, the walks from Stinchar Bridge in the previous section were in East Ayrshire. (Confusingly, South Ayrshire and East Ayrshire are separate councils, while 'Ayrshire' as a whole doesn't exist any more.) Arrive here from Trool or the Glenkens, and you think you're in ever remoter hill country. But the towns, cities and former coal pits of industrial Ayrshire lie just out of sight to the north. And this will be reflected, on any summer weekend, by the other walkers you'll meet: firstly, that there'll be some; and secondly, in their Ayrshire speech and phrases, which somehow seem to go with these rocks, lochans and gnarly grassland.

Loch Doon is southern Scotland's largest loch. At 9km long, it comes in just behind Windermere and Ullswater, although it's a mere pool compared with the lochs of the Scottish Highlands. Its two dams mean it's technically a reservoir, feeding into the Glenkens hydroelectricity scheme to the southeast. But its wooded shores and ruined castle, its osprey observatory and tea room, give the feel of natural wild water at all but the driest times of year. The rise in water level was only 9m – just enough, sadly, to flood its island castle, which accordingly has been moved onto the mainland. The island castle played an important part in Scotland's wars of independence; six centuries later, the loch hosted seaplanes and an aerial gunnery training range during World War I.

Unless you're from Ayrshire, Loch Doon isn't the natural first point of call. But it is the way in along the Gala Lane, below the grim east faces of the Dungeon range, towards the Dungeon Lochs and the fabled bottomless bog of the Silver Flowe. Okay, so the Gala Lane is clogged up with commercial spruce, the harsh forest tracks giving easy and uninteresting access even for cyclists right through the range to Loch Dee (see the return leg of Route 16). But this is also the way to get your feet onto the wonderful Hoodens Hill, northern outlier of Mullwharchar (Route 16 taken in the right direction). That can be combined with Route 17 to make a fine long circuit with a return along the Rhinns of Kells range. Meanwhile, Craiglee of Doon (Route 15) offers a shorter ascent to a picnic viewpoint high above the loch.

ROUTE 15
Craiglee of Doon

Start/finish	Loch Doon Castle (NX 483 949)
Distance	8km (5 miles)
Ascent	400m (1300ft)
Harshness	5
Approx time	3hr 30min
Terrain	Small path and grassy hillsides, but a very harsh forest ride on the descent
Highest point	Craiglee, 523m
Parking	Below the castle

Craiglee of Doon and Craiglee of Dee make a matched pair at the north and south of the main Galloway range. This Craiglee is a short ascent from Loch Doon, with grand views into the heart of the range. The preliminary Wee Hill of Craigmulloch has more intimate views down onto Loch Doon.

The descent southwards starts down a harsher side of the hill, with longer grass and granite knolls. And it finishes up with a pleasant forest path above the loch. But in between, there's a belt of forestry to be got through: in high summer especially, this is a very tough bit of ground with thigh-deep grasses and some bog myrtle. A simple up-and-down to Craiglee, or just to its preliminary Wee Hill, may well be preferred then.

From the car park, cross to a clear path, marked Craiglea [*sic*] Trail, up to the left of the **castle** ruins. The path runs up through woods to a forest road. Cross to the continuing path, which runs up northwest in a gap between plantations, to the right of a small stream. It gets fainter as it turns directly uphill, north, emerging on heathery slopes to reach the plateau of **Wee Hill of Craigmulloch**. ▶ It's worth turning right, to a corner poised above Loch Doon, before heading gently up short heather to the summit cairn.

A Scots–Gaelic tautology, meaning the small hill of the craggy hill of the summit.

WALKING THE GALLOWAY HILLS

Another tautology – local term 'nick' and Gaelic mam both mean a pass.

Slopes of fairly short heather lead down to the grassy saddle of Nick of the Mahm. ◀ A small path is just about findable across the damp saddle and up the shaggily grassy slope of **Craiglee**. The higher part of the hill is pleasant going, with some rock peeping through the grass and heather. There's a cairn, then a trig point.

Descend southwest, aiming for distant Loch Macaterick and Kirriereoch Hill directly above it. Soon you pass onto the granite ground, with occasional rounded slabs among the grasses. For best going, keep to the tops of the granite knolls rather than the deeply grassy hollows between. As the slope eases, what looks like a clear path is actually a stream; follow the slightly higher ground just to its right. At NX 4660 9539 you could come across a wooden memorial cross.

Craiglee and Wee Hill of Craigmulloch above Loch Doon

The stream enters plantations with clear-fell on its right (west) and growing trees on its left. Head down the tree gap to the left of the stream, with a fence and faint traces of path. Where fence and stream diverge, it's better to continue to the left of the fence. Here, at the time of writing, there are mature, open trees to your right; there may be easier passage through these than along the grassy ride.

After the stream and fence rejoin, the ride becomes very tough going indeed, with thigh-deep grass. It's important to conserve effort, and patience, for this 700-metre stage of the walk. ▶

At last you emerge onto the smooth track of the Carrick Forest Drive. Turn left, above **Carrick Lane**, to a junction (with **car park** below) at the head of Loch Doon. At this point, those feeling lively will take the other end of the Craiglee/Craiglea Trail on a path that sets off uphill to the left, marked with a waymark post. (Those feeling tired can carry on along the smooth track, which becomes tarmac then arrives at Loch Doon Castle. The slightly less tired can take the forest track forking up left just after the waymarked path.)

Clear-felling on the right, likely to happen by the early 2020s, will alter the character of this ride – presumably for the better as it's hard to conceive of its being worse.

The waymarked path wanders uphill, past a black bench made of recycled plastic, then zigzags back left. This leads to a high viewpoint above the loch head and another black bench. Backtrack for 75 metres, and keep ahead at the same level on a much fainter path, rather overgrown. It soon crosses a duckboard bridge, and continues level and roughly north, before gently descending northeast towards Wee Hill of Craigmulloch. ▶

If the path should be lost, making a way downhill will get you onto the forest track not far below.

The path crosses a stream and turns uphill for a few steps into a forest ride. It contours along this to another stream. Here, the path turns uphill, but head downhill instead. The deep grass and bog myrtle will bring unhappy memories of the descent of Craiglee – but this time it's for just 20 harsh metres to join the forest track just below. Follow it to the left for a few steps, before turning down the path used at the start of the walk, which returns you to the **car park**.

LOCH DOON CASTLE

Originally on an island in the middle of the loch, the castle was moved stone by stone to its present position when the rising reservoir flooded its island. It was built either by King Robert the Bruce or by his father as Earl of Carrick. It was surrendered to the English during the War of Independence (see Route 3) but recaptured in 1314. Besieged by the English in 1335 after the disastrous battle of Halidon Hill near Berwick, it was one of only five to stand firm for Scotland – the resistance of the five castles assuring the survival of the recently independent nation.

The castle was successfully besieged in 1511 in a local dispute between Kennedys and Douglases. It was deliberately destroyed in the 1520s by James V to reduce the powers of the local barons. The portcullis was thrown into the loch; 21st-century divers have tried, but failed, to trace it.

ROUTE 16
Hoodens Hill and Mullwharchar

Start/finish	Head of Loch Doon: junction of Forest Drive (NX 476 942)
Distance	24km (15 miles)
Ascent	950m (3000ft)
Harshness	5
Approx time	7hr 30min
Terrain	Rock-and-grass ridges and hilltops; rough moorland over Craigmawhannal (especially on the descent) and 500 metres of soggy tussocks in forest rides on the return
Highest point	Mullwharchar, 692m
Parking	Past Loch Doon Castle, in 800 metres the road becomes gravel track; in a further 600 metres, the Forest Drive is ahead and there's a car park on the track forking down left. The bridge over Carrick Lane ahead is marked 'no unauthorised traffic'.
Variants	Shortcut omitting Dungeon Hill: 21km (13 miles) with 800m (2700ft) ascent – about 6hr. Continuation combining this route with Route 17 gives a fine circuit of 32.5km (20½ miles) with 1600m (5300ft) ascent – about 11hr. For cyclists: riding to the track junction southeast of Craigmawhannal lets you access the foot of Hoodens Hill via the well-made footbridge at NX 469 902.

This is a route that encapsulates both the best and the worst of Galloway hillwalking. The bad is the 9km stretch of forest road; the even worse is the short section south of Craigmawhannal on former plantations, now tussocks with ditches, and the 500 metres of soggy forest ride. The good is Hoodens Hill, with its northern ridgeline and plateau of grass and granite slabs; the visit to Loch Enoch's little beach; and the granite slabs and grass of Dungeon Hill and the Brishie.

The variant descent directly from Mullwharchar is an escape route to shorten the walk, but it does leave out almost half of the really nice ground, including the excellent little ridge of the Brishie.

Mullwharchar, Hoodens Hill, Merrick and Kirriereoch Hill seen from Craigmawhannal

Follow the track over **Carrick Lane** and past Starr house on your left. In another 800 metres, take a track forking up to the right in trees. ◄ After 800 metres, fork off left, southwest. At the track end, keep ahead on faint wheelmarks through a tree gap onto the slopes of Craigmawhannal. The faint wheelmarks continue for a few hundred metres just above the forest edge. When the wheelmarks end, head uphill to the highest point of **Craigmawhannal**.

> A boulder just beyond this junction is provocatively marked 'Man – or Marmot?'

Ahead is a wide level plateau of soggy ground. Head round to the right of this on slightly higher ground. Then head down southwest into some nasty ground, former plantation burnt and not replanted. Below is a grove of dead trees; head down the edge of these. Pass to the left of the furthest-to-right dead tree to pick up a wheelmark track. This runs down through a gap in an old fence. It continues across a rough saddle and starts up the north ridgeline of Hoodens Hill.

The ridge is very pleasant with granite slabs, sculptural boulders and short grass. Head straight up it on a faint path to a cairn at the 546m spot height. The flat ridge beyond has a couple of unhelpful cairns. ◄ A small cairn marks **Hoodens Hill** summit.

> If it's not cloudy you won't need them, and if it is cloudy you won't see them.

Drop south, still on rocky slabby ground, to cross a saddle below. Pass between the two **lochans** and you could pick up a very small path. A slight shoulder is followed by a steeper slope up to **Mullwharchar** summit cairn.

Route 16 – Hoodens Hill and Mullwharchar

Direct descent to Gala Lane

The direct descent off Mullwharchar saves about an hour, but at a sad cost of omitting Loch Enoch and the Dungeon. Descend south, swinging left (southeast) as the slope eases and joining **Pulskaig Burn**. If the water level is low, bare rock alongside the stream gives easiest going. Just above the valley floor, cross the burn and keep northeast,

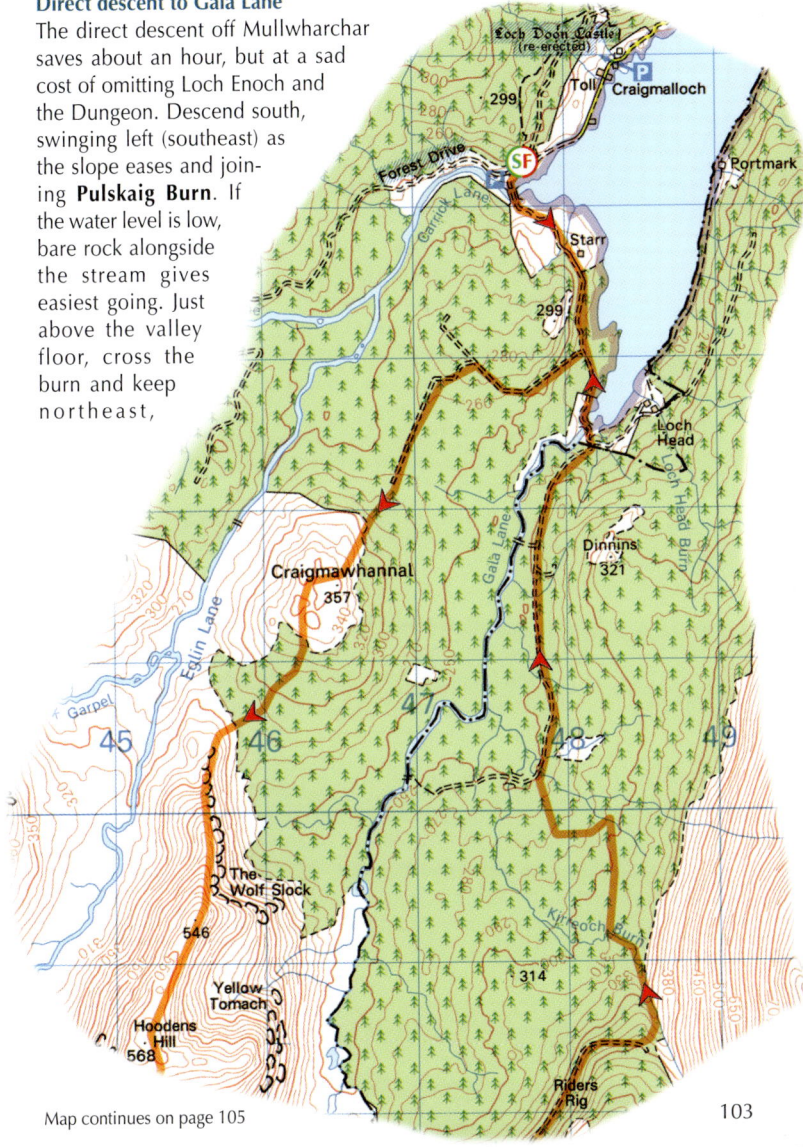

Map continues on page 105

easing away from it, to cross the head of **Gala Lane** opposite the gap into the plantations on the main route.

Descend just west of south, aiming for the sandy beach at the left (northeast) corner of **Loch Enoch**. This line gives not-bad rocky going across the flatter ground below. From the beach, slant up the slope of grass and rocks above the loch, enjoying the great views of Merrick, to reach the rocky top and cairn of **Craignairny**. Head north of east, with steeper ground dropping to your right, to the final rise to **Dungeon Hill**.

> At 610m, **Dungeon Hill** is the lowest 2000-footer in Scotland, and so counts as the country's smallest mountain. Despite that, its position right at the centre of the rugged Galloway Highlands means that it takes 3hr 30min of hard walking to reach it either southwards from Loch Doon or northwards from Loch Trool. This is roughly the time it takes to reach Ben Nevis (1345m) from its car park at Achintee.

Descend north, aiming for the level ridgeline ahead. After 200 metres, there's a short, sharp drop. Zigzag down on grass between granite lumps. Then set out along the level ridgeline north, with some bare rock for walking on and faint traces of path. As the ridgeline starts downwards, it takes the name Brishie. It gets steeper as it goes down, until its final steep drop-off above Gala Lane. Here, ease down to the left to take rough grass slopes just to the left of the ridgeline's steep terminus, onto gentler ground below.

Now below the Brishie, head down the moorland crest northeast to reach and cross a boggy little stream (the head of **Gala Lane**) opposite a gap in the plantations. ◄ Follow the gap between plantation blocks up to a forest road, which is met at the point where it forks.

The shortcut route rejoins here.

High-level return over Corserine
Combining the route over Mullwharchar with a return along the northern Rhinns of Kells gives a magnificent long outing of two quite different halves. The tree gap that

ROUTE 16 – HOODENS HILL AND MULLWHARCHAR

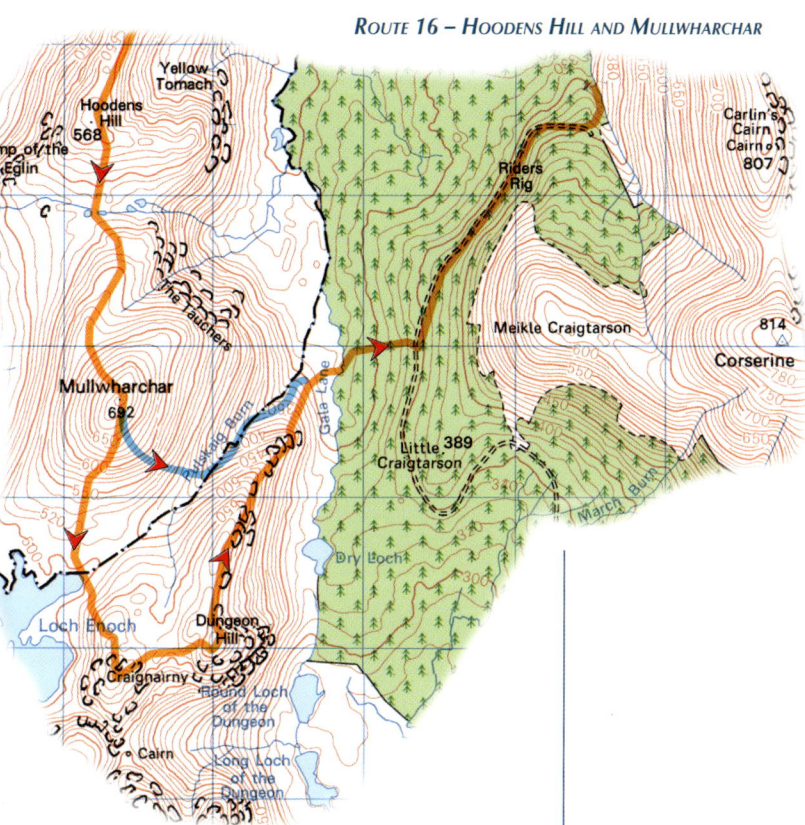

reached the track junction continues directly ahead, through very deep grass with mature trees to the right and clear-fell with new (mid 2010s) plantings to the left. The ascent of this is short, but very rough. Once above the plantations, continue steeply onto **Meikle Craigtarson**. The route is now the reverse of Route 17, continuing on the clear ridgelines over **Corserine**, **Meaul** and **Coran of Portmark** (refer to Route 17 map).

After descending Coran's northwest ridge to the forest top, ignore the path marked on Landranger maps, which doesn't exist. Instead, at Polmeadow Burn, contour left beside a broken wall for 500 metres to find the start of a forest track ahead. It leads to **Loch Head** to rejoin the outward route.

For the shorter way home, from the track junction head north on the upper fork, and follow it for 2km, round onto the north flank of **Riders Rig**. ◄ As the track bends right just before its end, a bulldozed quad-bike path starts immediately below. This wanders down through clear-fell, running about 50 metres up left of **Kirreoch Burn**. It passes stone-walled enclosures, to a ford of the burn (NX 4826 8918) leading directly into a wide ride (tree gap) running north.

The lower fork leads to a longer, soggier passage through the plantations.

The ride is fairly dry and has a faint path. This path may become more marked as people catch on that this is the best way of linking the two forest track systems from south and north. After 750 metres, it arrives at a smooth-surfaced forest track.

Turn left, southwest at first, but soon bending round to run northwest. Keep ahead at a track T-junction, and follow the track north for rather a long way, until **Loch Doon** appears ahead and you arrive at the track junction of the outward route. Okay, it's 2.5km of track – but you'd rather

On the south slope of Mullwharchar, with Loch Enoch and Merrick behind

ROUTE 16 – HOODENS HILL AND MULLWHARCHAR

I hadn't told you that. Turn left over Gala Lane and along above the loch to the **car park** at the walk start.

HIGH-LEVEL NUCLEAR WASTE

In 1978 there was a plan to dispose of the highest-level nuclear waste from the UK's power stations by sinking it in a 1500m shaft drilled into Mullwharchar. The idea was that the granite, being 200 million years old, might be expected to remain stable for the 100,000 years or so needed for the radioactivity to decay. The other idea was that Mullwharchar was a small hill that nobody had ever heard of.

The campaign against the proposal included a 100,000-signature petition, and a campaign song (composed by young activist Kathleen Stewart):

> My friend Mullwharchar, beloved over all
> To some a mountain, to others a hill
> Where shepherds and sinners bless the weather
> Caledonian homeland for ever!

And whether it was down to the song or the signatures, the proposal was rejected, in favour of leaving the stuff lying around at Sellafield in Cumbria for some future generation to sort out.

WALKING THE GALLOWAY HILLS

ROUTE 17
Northern Rhinns of Kells from Loch Doon

Start/finish	Head of Loch Doon: junction of Forest Drive (NX 476 942)
Distance	25.5km (16 miles)
Ascent	1000m (3300ft)
Harshness	4
Approx time	8hr
Terrain	Forest tracks, grassy hill ridges, and three short sections of rank vegetation in plantations
Highest point	Corserine, 814m
Parking	As Route 16
Variants	Using a bike to the Gala Lane bridge takes nearly an hour off the walk time

The northern Rhinns of Kells ridge provides a rising sequence from Coran of Portmark over Bow and Meaul, then Carlin's Cairn with its fine Bronze Age stonepile, to Corserine, Galloway's second peak, which is only 30m lower than Merrick itself. The ridge just gets better and better; the contrasting views are eastward to the green Glenkens, and westwards into the granite heartland with its various lochs and crags.

The downside is a certain amount of low-level stuff through the plantations at the walk's beginning and end. Of the three sections of pathless plantation, the first, along to Polmeadow Burn, is shorter than the map suggests due to extension of the forest road here. The third, joining the northern and southern track systems, is also greatly shortened by a well-built quad-bike path. But the middle one, at the foot of Meikle Craigtarson, has enough nastiness for all three, with grass that in August can be thigh-high. The affliction is brief, and the prize for it is worthwhile!

The track leads down across **Carrick Lane**, and south to the head of Loch Doon. Here, you cross **Gala Lane** to a junction just beyond. Continue on the track ahead, which bends round to the left to head down the loch in

ROUTE 17 – NORTHERN RHINNS OF KELLS FROM LOCH DOON

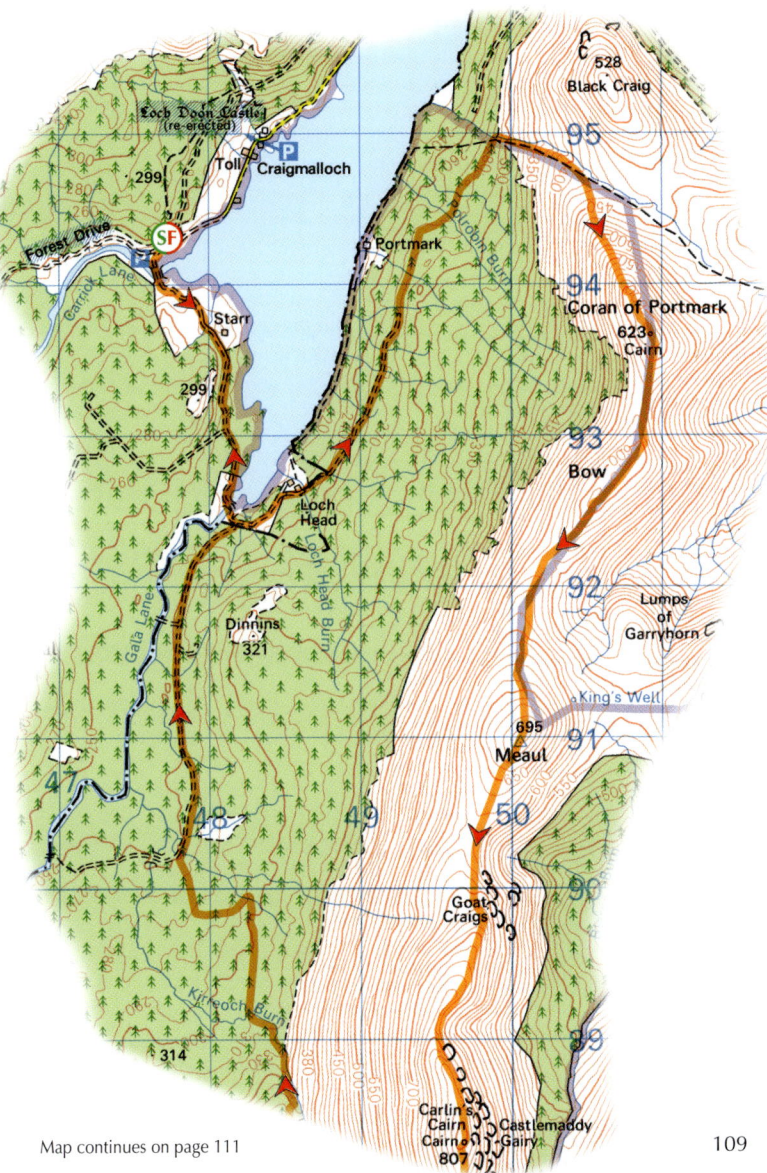

WALKING THE GALLOWAY HILLS

> A lochside path marked on Landranger maps does not exist and the going down there is not enjoyable.

plantations. ◀ Clear-felling above the track gives views to the hill slopes, but full-grown trees still conceal the loch below.

The track continues further than marked on current maps, crossing **Polrobin Burn**. Where it currently ends (NX 496 946), an old wall is just above. Continue above this wall, on faint track marks, to emerge from the plantation at Polmeadow Burn (unnamed on Landranger maps, it's the boundary of the forest park).

Turn uphill on the near side of the burn. The vegetation is rich and deep, especially in August. ◀ Soon you pass some small waterfalls, and the going gets easier. Head up to the right of a wall and then a fence, then bend up right to follow the northwest spur of **Coran of Portmark**. You may find a faint quad-bike track. Above, the ridge is pleasantly grassy, with a broken fence guiding up to Coran's summit.

> The August reward is the heather in flower, and a plentiful crop of bilberries.

Descend gently south across a saddle, and up to the first and higher cairn of **Bow**. The decayed fence continues southwest past the second top, just 1m lower, and across a saddle with a tiny pool. The north slope of Meaul has rougher, calf-deep plantlife. Keep uphill south, slanting away from the fence on your left, as the going becomes mildly rocky underfoot to **Meaul** trig point.

A faint path descends southwest to a col with small pools. You can just follow the rounded ridge crest onwards, but the path passes to the left of all the pools and heads up on the left (east) flank of the ridge with good views eastwards. It rejoins the ridgeline above **Goat Craigs**. Follow the attractive ridgeline gently uphill, along a level section, then gently rising again to the top of **Carlin's Cairn**.

> The huge **cairn** is Bronze Age, but somewhat messed about by later visitors. It is supposed to mark a grant of land by King Robert the Bruce to the wife (or carlin) of Polmaddie Mill. In Bruce's rambles in Galloway, she loyally hid him under some sacks of meal behind the mill wheel.

Historically minded readers may have noted that Bruce's campaign did not take place in the Bronze Age. Accordingly, at least one of these Carlin's Cairn claims has to be spurious.

Descend south, to cross a gentle (but steep-sided) col and up to the trig point on **Corserine**. Turn west, bending down left (southwest) as the slope steepens, and cross the plateau of **Meikle Craigtarson**. ▶ The plateau is a place of rocky knolls, with the one of them that might be considered as the summit having a knee-high rowan tree struggling against wind and wild goats. A cairn is at the northwest corner of the plateau. From it, head down the bumpy northwest spur. Follow this down into a bay of unplanted ground at the ridge foot.

Heading up Carlin's Cairn north ridge

The Gaelic original will have been Creag Tharsuinn Mhor, the large transverse crag.

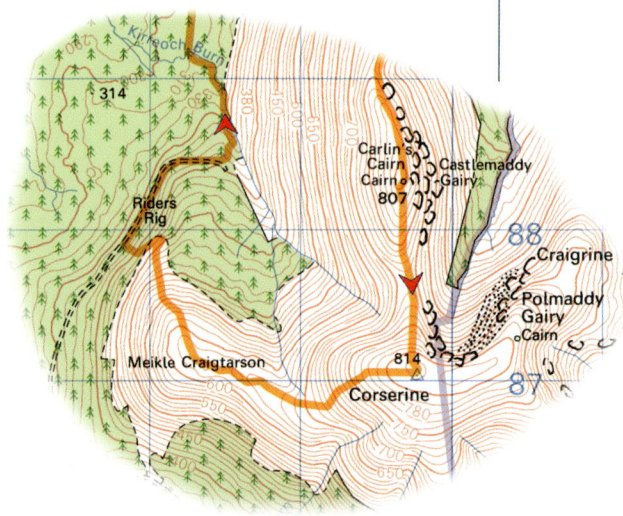

WALKING THE GALLOWAY HILLS

Carlin's Cairn from the slopes of Corserine

At the point where the first trees are on your right, the tree gap you want is down to the left (NX 4793 8784). However, the ground directly above the tree gap is very steep. So head along the top of the steep ground to the back corner of the unplanted bay, then double back left along the top of the plantation. The tree gap, soft and peaty surfaced, heads down to the forest track just below. (If your patience fails, just head straight down between the trees at any likely point, as the forest track is close below. The wide tree gap marked on Explorer maps does not exist; the actual gap is 150 metres southwest.)

Turn right, to work around the **Riders Rig**. Here, the track bends eastwards, with views over the clear-fell towards the Dungeon Hills. As the track bends right again, just before its end, a bulldozed quad-bike path starts immediately below. This wanders down through clear-fell, running about 50 metres up left of **Kirreoch Burn**. It passes stone-walled enclosures, to a ford of the burn (NX 4826 8918) leading directly into a wide ride (tree gap) running north.

The ride is fairly dry and has a faint path. After 750 metres, it arrives at a smooth-surfaced forest track. Turn left, southwest at first, but soon bending round to run northwest. Keep ahead at a track T-junction, and follow the track north for 2.5km, until **Loch Doon** appears ahead and you arrive at the track junction of the outward route. Turn left over **Gala Lane** and along above the loch to the **car park** at the walk start.

SECTION 4: THE GLENKENS

Corserine from Meikle Lump (Route 22)

INTRODUCTION

The western end of the Southern Uplands is split by several wide valleys which run south to north from the Solway right through to the lowlands of Ayrshire. This was a system of rift valleys from the break-up of the Pangaea supercontinent, regouged for the present day by southward glaciers from the Highland ice cap. (The other former rift valleys are the nearly linked Stranraer sea lochs in the west, Nithsdale and Annandale to the east.) The wide, green valley called the Glenkens is the major break in the range – the Southern Upland Way takes a full day to walk across it.

Back in the 1930s, the full length of the Water of Ken was adapted for hydroelectricity generation, with a series of dams giving three small lochs and then the long, narrow Loch Ken below New Galloway. The small scale of it all, along with the charmingly retro styling of the various works and power stations, means that the electricity scheme enhances rather than spoils the feel of the wide valley.

But the narrator of SR Crockett's novel *The Raiders* commiserates with its unhappy inhabitants. Its grassy slopes give no convenient hiding places for stolen cattle and smuggled brandy, so that the people have to live by boring old farming and lead mining.

Indeed, this east side of the range is grassy and gentler, without the rugged grandeur of Glen Trool. No need to complain, when the grassiness extends the full 13km of the grand Rhinns of the Kells, a classic ridgeline accessed in bits, or even complete, from Forrest Lodge (Routes 21 and 22). The couthy (pleasant and comfortable) Glenkens also offers accommodation and shops accessible by bus and right alongside the hills. Carsphairn in particular is for the car-free, with Cairnsmore of Carsphairn (Route 19) and the Kells ridge (Route 18) right beside the village.

And finally, the wide valley floor itself offers small and pleasant hillwalks for a summer evening or a sharp winter's day. The little, rounded Mulloch and Waterside Hills above Dalry (Routes 23 and 24), approached by pastureland tracks, riversides and oakwoods, could not be more different from the harsh wee mini-mountains above Loch Trool... even if Dunveoch Hill (Route 25) does offer a surprise scrambling opportunity.

ROUTE 18

Garryhorn and the northern Rhinns of Kells

Start/finish	Bridge-end farm, 1.5km north of Carsphairn (NX 557 943)
Distance	16km (10 miles)
Ascent	750m (2500ft)
Harshness	4
Approx time	5hr 30min
Terrain	Tracks, grassy slopes and ridges; rough moorland below Cairnsgarroch
Highest point	Meaul summit, 695m
Parking	On fragment of old road, between road and river on south side of bridge over Water of Deugh

This is a fairly short day out on the northern end of the Rhinns of Kells. Along the way, there's a chance to rest your buttocks on the stone sat on by King Robert the Bruce in 1307; there are great views of the central hills and Loch Doon from the gentle grassy ridgeline, and an instructive visit to the UK's best-preserved old mine flue and chimney. There's a short section of rough moorland below Cairnsgarroch and on the descent from Coran of Portmark; the tops themselves are good, grassy going.

Cairnsmore of Carsphairn from the track above Garryhorn

WALKING THE GALLOWAY HILLS

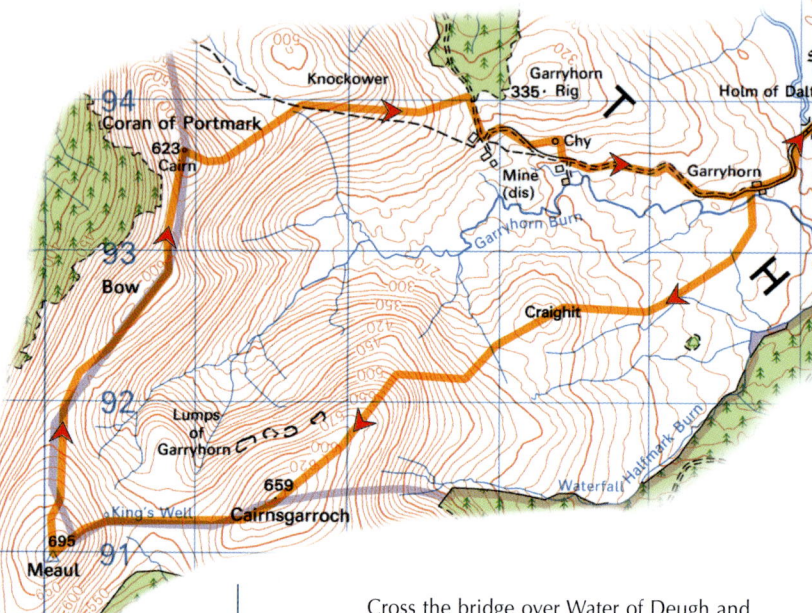

Cross the bridge over Water of Deugh and take the tarmac track on the left signed for **Holm of Daltallochan**. The track passes that farm and crosses the level valley floor and Carsphairn Lane stream. Then it becomes gravelled and rises to **Garryhorn**, a white stone farm cluster with big sycamore trees. Just after the buildings, take a rough track down left through two gates to ford Garryhorn Burn. The track rambles across grassy moorland through a gate and southwest. Where it bends south, keep ahead, past a circular sheep stell, then head up west onto the low but somewhat rocky **Craighit**.

Craighit is formed of **conglomerate**, or puddingstone: the normally featureless greywacke rock here contains larger chunks and lumps of up to 10cm, a bit like the nuts and raisins in a Christmas pudding. While ordinary greywacke is formed from mudslides off the edge of a continental shelf, this represents a more serious slide also involving broken-up

ROUTE 18 – GARRYHORN AND THE NORTHERN RHINNS OF KELLS

bits of the underlying bedrock. The resulting puddingstone is even tougher than ordinary greywacke. It also forms the projecting ridge of Cairnsgarroch, next in this walk, and the small but lumpy Craig of Knockgray (Route 20) on the other side of the Glenkens.

Head southwest, over rough grassland with tussocks and rushes, to cross a fence. ▶ As the slope steepens, the going improves. Slant up to the right, to reach gentler slopes above. Head up southwest to the Shepherd's Cairn, where you join a broken wall, with **Cairnsgarroch** summit cairn just beyond, to the left of the wall.

Follow the decayed wall down to a wide saddle, where it's joined by a decayed fence. As the slope steepens, and just below where another fence joins from the left, contour out to the right for 75 metres to find the **King's Well** and Stone.

There are in fact three stones for sitting down on, and it's hard to decide which of them **King Robert the Bruce** would have found most comfortable during his guerrilla campaign of 1307. The Well is a tiny mossy spring, a reliable water source.

Slant up left to rejoin the wall, and follow it to its top. Continue uphill gently southwest to **Meaul**'s trig point. ▶ Descend north, with Loch Doon gleaming ahead and below. Soon join a broken fence, with a quad-bike track on its left. On the gentlest of grassy going, the ridge bends right and rises to **Bow**, with a cairn at either end, the further one being 1m higher. The fence and path then run slightly down left of the following saddle, for better views down to Loch Doon, then rise to **Coran of Portmark**.

A gateway seen up left is in a crossing fence and doesn't get you across the one you need to cross.

For those familiar with the main Scottish Highlands, the name's derivation is obvious: it's Gaelic Meall, or hump.

Descend southeast for 200 metres, to the top of a broad spur running down east at first, then more gently northeast. Keep to the exact crest of the spur, where you should find faint quad-bike wheelmarks which will become crucial for the crossing of the rough moorland below. ◄ The quad-bike track runs just down to the right of the **Knockower** saddle and above the very head of a stream, then slants down just south of east. Soon there is a fence just below it. The wheelmarks take you down to a saddle at the top of a plantation. Here, you turn right on a rough track through a spacious kissing gate and down into the former Garryhorn mines.

At a set of roofless ruins, turn left onto a clearer track through ground poisoned with lead mine tailings. After 500 metres, contour off left through very rough grassland to visit the tall chimney ruin (**Chy** on the OS map). Descend alongside the stone-built sunken flue to rejoin the track below, just above the former smelting works.

The track runs down the valley to **Garryhorn farm**, continuing past **Holm of Daltallochan** to the walk start.

> The path marked on OS maps was a medieval highway to Loch Doon Castle, but no longer exists on the ground.

MINES AT GARRYHORN

The Woodhead Mine here opened around 1840, with pumps and crushers powered by water from the hill streams. For the next 30 years it was a flourishing concern supporting 300 people living in the high valley, with a school and a non-conformist church (Lamloch Kirk).

Smelting gases with sulphates and lead were known even then as being poisonous. Accordingly they were carried uphill in buried flues built of stone slabs, and released above the working areas in the chimneys whose ruins are the most spectacular feature of the former mine area.

Flue with a flaw: Garryhorn mine chimney

ROUTE 19
Cairnsmore of Carsphairn

Start/finish	Bridge-end farm, 1.5km north of Carsphairn (NX 557 943)
Distance	17km (10½ miles)
Ascent	750m (2500ft)
Harshness	3
Approx time	5hr 45min
Terrain	Track, grassy slopes and smooth plateau, riverbank finish
Highest point	Cairnsmore summit, 797m
Parking	On fragment of old road, between road and river on south side of bridge over Water of Deugh
Variants	Down over Dunool: 11.5km (7¼ miles) with 650m (2200ft) ascent – about 4hr

Rising just east of the Glenkens valley, Cairnsmore of Carsphairn is not part of the Galloway Hills as such – although it is of course a hill, and does stand in Galloway. It's included here as one of the area's four Corbetts, the 2500-footers. Also, if the granite of Loch Enoch is the group's distinctive rock, Cairnsmore is the highest summit made of granite.

Cairnsmore is a sprawling, grassy hump, sprinkled over its higher slopes with rounded boulders. With a good track giving access to the hill, and fairly smooth slopes above, the hill presents little difficulty and only a modicum of excitement. But its freestanding position gives it wide and beautiful views of the Rhinns of Kells, the Glenkens valley, and the grassy hills extending eastwards. The route here includes a section of riverbank past Carsphairn. To deprive yourself of this pleasure, as well as the side summit Beninner, there's a short descent by Dunool.

Cross the A713 to the track through Bridge-end farm – there's a Core Path sign at the track end. Past the farm, ignore a new track to the right under power lines. The older track passes above a pool above the river, the **Green Well of Scotland**.

The **Green Well of Scotland** is somewhat surprising, since the pool is perched well above the river alongside. Legend has it as a pagan holy site taken over as a baptismal pool by early Christians. Polluted from the farm track above, it wouldn't be advised for dunkings today.

Route 19 – Cairnsmore of Carsphairn

The track passes above a corner of the river, and drops to riverside flats past a shed. At 500 metres from the farm, the track becomes mucky past another shed to a gate. ▶ The track rises above the river, and heads northeast along the slopes of **Willieanna** and **Dunool**. On the slopes of Dunool, the first small granite outcrops are seen.

You could cross the fence on the left to the riverside to avoid any track mud.

The track ends against a stone wall, and a faint path runs up to the right of this. The wall bends right, for a level soggy section, then back left to cross a stream, with a small and unnecessary footbridge. The path continues uphill to the right of the wall, quite steeply, passing among some boulders. It crosses a level shoulder before steepening again through stonefields to the summit trig point and cairn of **Cairnsmore of Carsphairn**.

The interpretation board at Green Well claims that from **Cairnsmore summit** there are views of Wales and Ireland – not visible from here, says the computer, although the Lake District and Isle of Man can be. An anemometer on the summit (February 2018) had recorded a wind speed of 'too strong'; the rotor was bent over, almost touching the ground.

Head east of south across the plateau, with steep drops to your left. As the ground starts to drop ahead, a fence arrives from the right.

Descent by Dunool

This shortcut has comfortable grassy going all the way, but misses out the riverside ending. Turn right along the fence. It runs out down the gentle ridge to **Black Shoulder**, where it becomes a wall. The wall runs down rather steeply, to the level shoulder of **Dunool**. Here are granite boulders for resting on, and a small cairn to the right of the wall.

West slopes of Cairnsmore of Carsphairn, with Dunool behind

Down from the small cairn, just above where the wall bends down left, there's a ramshackle stile. Use it if necessary to cross to the right (north) side of the wall. Go down steeply alongside the wall to the dip before Willieanna. Here, a fence runs down to the right – it could be followed to rejoin the ascent track. Otherwise keep ahead through a gateway and up to the right of the wall over **Willieanna**. ◀ Descend west, slanting away from the wall, to join the ascent track at a gate in a lower wall. Retrace the outward route back to the walk start.

The minor summit is actually on the left side of the wall but would require a climb over it and back.

For Beninner, cross a simple stile at the near corner of the fence, then go down the bouldery slope to the right of the fence, to a wide col. Here, another fence crosses, with another small stile. Then a faint path leads up to the cairn on **Beninner**.

Head down the wide grassy ridgeline south. The ground gets rougher and steepens as you head down to the left of a fence to the base of Knockwhirn. Go through a gate and head up Knockwhirn, to the right of a derelict fence.

Cross the top of **Knockwhirn**. ◀ Continue to the right of what's now a derelict wall and head down towards Benloch Burn. When the wall bends away left, continue straight down aiming towards a rectangular pine plantation, to find a gate in a crossing fence. Head straight

Step across the ruined fence if you want to visit the actual, insignificant highest point of it.

down rough ground to find (if lucky) quad-bike wheelmarks to the left of the stream. Once past the plantation that's on the other side of the stream, the wheelmarks cross **Benloch Burn** and wander across moorland to the right of it, before returning to the stream and the start of a stony track. Recross the stream on this, and follow it as it rambles southwest. Ignore a fainter side track to the right as the main track bends left and wanders generally south to reach **Knockgray**.

Go through a gate and turn right on a wider track, through another gate. Follow the track ahead to join the **B729**. Turn right, to a road junction in front of a war memorial (**Meml** on map). Turn right on the old main road, past a couple of houses, to join the A713. A footpath to the right of the road leads into **Carsphairn**.

Towards the end of the village, just after Kirkholm B&B, a short track bears left between houses to a field gate. ▶ Continue on a faint grass track to the river. Follow it upstream, continuing along a second field to its corner. Here, turn back sharp right along a wall to a gate onto the **A713**. Turn left along the road, then left on a fragment of older road past a house. Where the old road rejoins the A713, cross a fence on the left, to find more old road buried within the woodland, leading to the parking place at the walk start.

For more detailed description, see the start of Route 20.

Cairnsmore of Carsphairn seen from Waterside Hill on Route 24

ROUTE 20
Craig of Knockgray

Start/finish	Carsphairn (NX 561 932)
Alternative Start/finish	Liggat (NX 568 931)
Distance	7.5km (4½ miles)
Ascent	200m (700ft)
Harshness	3 (or 2 for the shorter route from Liggat)
Approx time	2hr 15min
Terrain	Rough pasture, tracks, grassy riverbank
Highest point	Craig of Knockgray, 383m
Parking	Street parking in Carsphairn
Variants	A shorter route from Liggat avoids the awkward wall crossing at the summit: 3.5km (2 miles) with 200m (700ft) ascent – about 1hr 15min

This small hill immediately above Carsphairn has grand views of the Glenkens, Rhinns of Kells and Cairnsmore. The top is slightly rocky, and the descent features an unexpected graveyard in a wood. The hill can be combined with a riverside walk by the Water of Deugh and a visit to Carsphairn's tea room and tiny heritage centre.

A wall crossing at the hill's summit needs care and agility (I've asked D&G Council for a ladder stile, but budgets are very tight). A shorter route from Liggat, east of Carsphairn, avoids this; on the main route there's also an alternative descent in case you get there and then decide against the wall climb.

Towards the north end of the village, just after Kirkholm B&B, a short track bears left between houses to a field gate. Continue on a faint grass track to the **Water of Deugh**. Follow the river upstream, past its confluence with Carsphairn Lane, and round the end of a wall. Follow the edge of a second field to its corner. Here, turn back sharp right along the wall to a gate onto the **A713**.

ROUTE 20 – CRAIG OF KNOCKGRAY

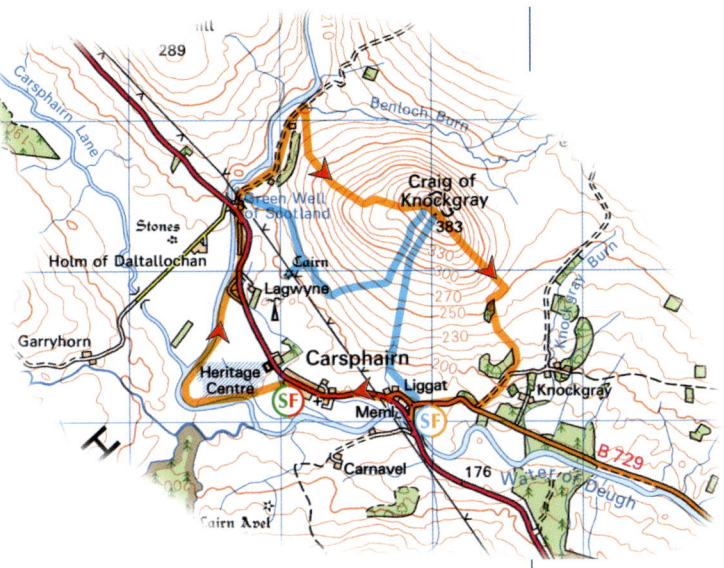

Turn left along the verge, walking on top of concrete flood-defence blocks, then left on a fragment of old road past a house. Where this old road rejoins the A713, turn left into woods to pass round the end of a fence. Buried within the wood strip you soon find that some more old road runs forward to rejoin the A713 near its bridge over Water of Deugh. ▶

Car parking place here.

Cross to the track past Bridge-end farm, passing above **Green Well of Scotland**. After 750 metres, you have passed one shed to a gate just beyond a second shed. Through this, take a gate on the right onto the hill foot. Turn back right to go up to the left of a fence, above the shed just passed and up the wide spur of **Craig of Knockgray**. Follow this fence to a high wall at the hill's summit. The best place to cross is right at the top, squeezing behind a strainer post to climb the corner behind, emerging on the right in the south-facing quadrant. It's a sheltered wall corner with the summit cairn just below.

Alternative descents

For a shorter, easier and less interesting descent, head south to the left of the wall to a mobile phone mast. Below, continue down to a power pylon and the war memorial at **Liggat**, there rejoining the main route to Carsphairn.

It may be, however, that you have failed to achieve the contortions to cross the rather forbidding summit wall. In this case, descend to the right of the wall until just above the mobile phone mast. Slant down to the right to find a field gate, and a track built during the construction of a line of power pylons just below.

Turn right, and pass a spur track to a pylon on your left. To visit the ancient Lagwine Cairn, which can be seen below, take the second pylon spur. Go through a gate behind the pylon and turn down left, past a stone sheep stell, to the sprawling ancient **cairn**. ◀ Return and continue along the track past another pylon spur and above Bridge-end cottage to rejoin the outward route.

From **Craig of Knockgray** summit cairn, head down southeast to the right of a wall to the foot of the slope. With another wall crossing below, head to the right to the

> Originally more than 20 metres across, the cairn is still impressive even though many stones have been stolen.

Carsphairn and Rhinns of Kells, from Craig of Knockgray

top edge of a plantation, Cemetery Wood. A small gate leads into the wood to the small private cemetery of the Kennedys of Knockgray. A rough path leads down through the wood to exit through another small gate into a field.

Head downhill towards a wood, then bear left on tractor wheelmarks to a gate at the left corner of this wood. A muddy track runs down beside the wood and bends right along its lower edge, to meet the driveway of **Knockgray farm**. Turn down right, to the **B729**.

Turn right to a road junction in front of the war memorial at **Liggat**. Turn right past a couple of houses, to join the A713. A footpath beside the road runs into **Carsphairn**.

Shorter version from Liggat

For an even shorter outing, avoiding the awkward wall crossing at the top of Craig of Knockgray, start at the war memorial at **Liggat** (NX 568 931). A few steps up B729, a short track leads left to a power pylon. ▶ Head straight uphill, to the right of a wall, to pass a mobile phone mast and reach **Craig of Knockgray** summit. Descend as on the main route past Knockgray graveyard.

This power line is newer than, and uphill from, the one marked on OS maps.

WALKING THE GALLOWAY HILLS

ROUTE 21
Corserine from Forrest Lodge

Start/finish	Burnhead Bridge by Forrest Lodge (NX 553 862)
Distance	14.5km (9 miles)
Ascent	700m (2700ft)
Harshness	4
Approx time	5hr
Terrain	Forest tracks, fairly steep grassy slopes, level plateau
Highest point	Corserine, 814m
Parking	Estate car park (no overnight parking)
Variants	Route 22 extends this route southwards over Meikle Millyea

Seen from within the Galloway hill group, Corserine is a wide grassy hump. And that impression is confirmed if crossing the full Rhinns of Kells: the ridge's high point is one of its less interesting summits. But in the east, Corserine has a corrie of real drama, with steep grassy slopes interrupted by a swarm of little crags. From the exit point of the plantations, a small peaty path weaves up between the crags onto Craigrine. The descent by North Gairy Top is pathless, so needs a little care with the compass. It's also pretty steep.

The convenient car park provided by Forrest Estate reduces the plantation walk-in to just 4km – still rather more than we really wanted!

Leave the car park northwest on a track with a small 'path' signpost. This immediately joins with Birger Natvig Road, a wide, smooth forest track running west through open ground, with Lumford Burn nearby on its right, and what will be a wood of rowan trees (planted early 2010s) to the left.

The smooth track passes left of the house at **Fore Bush**, then rakes along the foot of a clear-felled slope. It re-enters plantations to a fork. Here, Robert Watson Road, to the right, is the direct way towards the hill but instead fork left for 400 metres. A track down right leads

North Gairy Top and Loch Harrow

across the dam of **Loch Harrow**, with Craigbrock, the walk's descent route, looking rather fearsome above.

Cross the dam and slipway to the dam's end. Take a faint and very rough track trace ahead, west, for 100 metres to a clearing with a leat or artificial stream. Follow the stream left to the loch shore. Turn right, crossing the leat outflow and another just beyond, then turn right up a track.

This rises past a hydro-turbine hut to a track junction. The crossing track is Robert Watson Road. Turn left, gently uphill. After 600 metres, the track bends right and a small rough track continues ahead, signed to 'stile over deer fence'. The track soon joins the leat that's the diverted Folk Burn, and runs to the left of it. After 500 metres, you reach the point where the leat and the former stream bed diverge. Here, a rough track continues to the left of the burn – this will be the descent route. The main track crosses the **Folk Burn** via a culvert, with another sign to 'stile over deer fence', and soon reaches the top edge of the forest. ▶

The heralded 'deer fence' is a low sheep fence and unmaintained, with the stile half decomposed.

The slope above is quite steep, with small crags dotted about. A very welcome small peaty path leads directly uphill. It passes to the left of a rocky knoll. As the ground steepens, the path goes up to the left of an easy-angled, vegetated crag: this can be rewardingly scrambled. With more small crags to the left and above, the path bends right above the top of the scrambly crag.

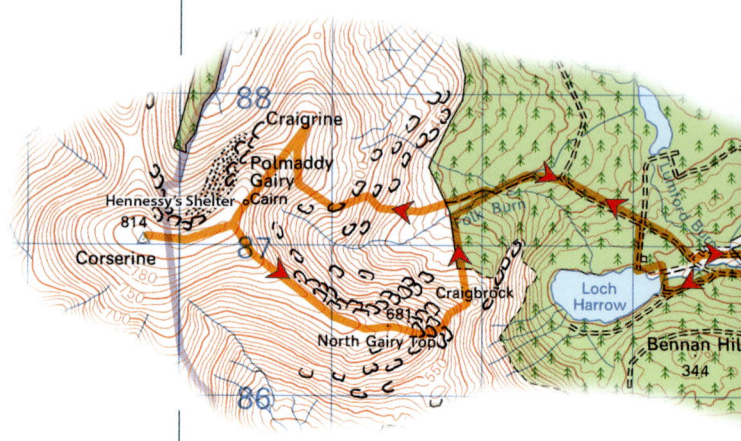

You are now on less steep and grassier ground, where the path is less needed and less well marked. It runs up roughly west. But as the ascent becomes easy at the 700m contour, it's rewarding to slant right, north, to the level shoulder of **Craigrine**. This has a small cairn just before the rock knoll that is its 709m spot height.

Note that if descending this route, the top of the small peaty path will be hard to find, requiring luck or else GPS: aim for NX 5129 8729 to find the path down between the little crags. There will be discomfort but no serious problems in descending the slope without finding the path. Enter plantations at Folk Burn, or at the old stile 100 metres north of it.

Cross the wide, level shoulder with some bare rock poking up, and ascend the wide grassy ridgeline southwest. On the eastern edge of the ridge is **Hennessy's Shelter**, a large shelter cairn. In another 200 metres, you reach a smaller cairn at the eastern end of Corserine's summit plateau. A small path leads west over almost level ground to the trig point at **Corserine** summit.

Route 21 – Corserine from Forrest Lodge

Return to the small cairn at the eastern end of the plateau. ▶ Descend a wide, rounded ridge southeast. It becomes a level shoulder leading to the small cairn on **North Gairy Top**. Descend east, passing another cairn, aiming for the right-hand edge of Loch Harrow. The ground becomes quite steep, with small crags, but the going is grassy between the outcrops.

As the slope eases (it gets much steeper again immediately below), slant down to the left, northeast, towards the very small rise of **Craigbrock**. Just before it, you reach a poorly maintained fence. Turn down left above it, soon with plantations below. Cross a decayed stile, as there are faint path traces between fence and forest. Follow the fence down to the **Folk Burn**.

Just before the stream, turn down right in a tree gap with a rough track. Soon you rejoin the rather better track used on the upward journey. Head down this less rough track, and keep ahead down Robert Watson Road past the junction where you joined it on the way up.

The next junction on the left is Caroline Currie Road, which you can use to vary the route. It fords a small stream, and heads downhill through plantations, up to the left of the stream. With a white turbine hut seen ahead, turn right, on a track which crosses the valley floor to the house at **Fore Bush**. Turn left on the track used for the upward journey. Just before the **car park**, keep ahead to visit the Black Watch statue at the lodge's gateway, then return to the car park.

| From here, you can see Hennessy's Shelter; if you have reached Hennessy's Shelter, you must backtrack.

FORREST ESTATE

Forrest Estate is owned by Fred Olsen, described as Norway's most radical billionaire, whose family shipping company has diversified to become a world player in renewable energy, specifically offshore wind farms. Like several other expatriate owners in Scotland, he runs his estate in an enlightened way, providing the useful car park, running micro-hydro schemes, and earning local loyalty as an employer. When reporters were chasing after some family scandal in the 1980s, locals enjoyed misdirecting them into futile journeys around the long forest tracks.

The figurehead at the lodge entrance is from the ship *Black Watch*, testament to the family's enthusiasm for Scotland – enthusiasm that was apparently not dented even when this ship (requisitioned by the Germans) was sunk by the Royal Navy's aircraft just two days before the end of World War II in Europe.

Black Watch figurehead, Forrest Lodge

ROUTE 22
Southern Rhinns of Kells

Start/finish	Burnhead Bridge by Forrest Lodge (NX 553 862)
Distance	19km (12 miles)
Ascent	950m (3200ft)
Harshness	3
Approx time	8hr
Terrain	Forest tracks, hillside with small path, grassy ridges; rugged path on descent
Highest point	Corserine, 814m
Parking	Estate car park (no overnight parking)

This is, quite simply, a first-rate hillwalk. The convenient car park at Forrest Lodge makes for only a moderate amount of forest trudge; then there's an interesting ascent to Corserine, followed by the fine ridgeline of the best part of the Kells range, over Millfire and Milldown. The only disappointment is not also including Carlin's Cairn.

Follow Route 21 to the summit of **Corserine**. ▶

Descend from the trig point south-southeast. Until Millfire is visible ahead, you need a compass (or GPS) line here. At 700m level, the ridgeline reforms, running south and then southeast, with plantations just below on the right. Keep close to drops on the left for the small path to the cairn on **Millfire**. The ridge runs level for 800 metres, then rises. Above this col, a wall crosses, and now walkers have a guiding wall along the ridgeline. The summit cairn of **Milldown** is to the left of the wall, above the steep drop to Loch Dungeon.

Wall and path run down through rugged ground to the small **Lochans of Auchniebut** before the final rise to **Meikle Millyea**. You arrive at a trig point and large ancient cairn. Harvey mapping has the true summit (749m) at the cairn 400 metres southwest, and it's a pleasant plateau

Ardent scramblers could instead ascend Corserine via Craigbrock to take advantage of easy-angled slabby rocks on the east end of North Gairy Top.

The summit, out to the left, has views across Loch Dungeon to Corserine.

wander out and back to visit it (also gaining southward views to Loch Dee).

From the main cairn and trig point, turn downhill northeast, soon joining a broken wall with path alongside. The wall levels off along the shoulder **Meikle Lump**. ◀ The wall and path bend down east for 600

ROUTE 22 – SOUTHERN RHINNS OF KELLS

metres, then bend 90 degrees left, to descend steeply northeast alongside a small stream.

Just above the forest fence, slant down left to a ladder stile into the trees. The ride ahead (blocked by a couple of fallen trees) leads in 200 metres to a forest track (Professor Heiberg Road). Turn down right, ignoring a side track on the left and passing an elevated wooden hide used for shooting roe deer. The track bends left (northeast) to a crossroads. Keep ahead, on a wide, smooth track, with cleared ground to the left allowing views to Cairnsmore of Carsphairn.

Keep following the main track ahead and downhill. It passes between two houses at **Burnhead**, and joins Burnhead Burn to arrive back at the **car park**.

Feral goats on Millfire

KELLS RANGE COMPLETE

The long, straight ridge of the Kells cries out to be completed in full. I did this once with a fellrunning friend using a car left in advance at Craigencallie behind Clatteringshaws Loch (NX 503 778). (The convenient finish is by a forest track southwest of Meikle Millyea.) Having enjoyed the full grandeur of the Kells range, we found that the keys of the return car had been securely locked away – in the boot of the arrival car, still at Green Well of Scotland. When asking friendly locals for help, it's better not to be wearing hillrunners' sky-blue Lycra tights…

Without car-key complications, the full range can be enjoyed by the energetic from Forrest Lodge, or rather less conveniently from Carsphairn. From Forrest Lodge, use forest tracks and a brief excursion through rides and clearings past the former Shiel of Castlemaddy bothy (NX 539 901). Emerge below the gorge of Halfmark Burn (NX 542 916) and cross Cairnsgarroch to Corserine, descending from Meikle Millyea as on Route 22. The full walk is 29km (18 miles) with 1300m (4400ft) ascent – about 9hr 30min.

Southern Rhinns of Kells and Loch Dee

ROUTE 23
Mulloch Hill

Start/finish	St John's Town of Dalry (NX 619 812)
Alternative Start/finish	A713 at Boat Knowe (NX 625 802)
Distance	5km (3¼ miles)
Ascent	120m (400ft)
Harshness	1
Approx time	1hr 30min
Terrain	Good paths and grassy fields
Highest point	Mulloch Hill, 170m
Parking	Dalry Main Street; or lay-by at Boat Knowe on A713
Variants	Starting at Boat Knowe lets you take refreshments at Dalry's Clachan Inn, halfway round the walk

This walk has two drawbacks. The riverside section is much too short; and we'd prefer Mulloch Hill to be quite a bit higher! Otherwise this is the ideal way to spend a summer's evening, with some grand views of the Rhinns of Kells to inspire you further and higher in days ahead.

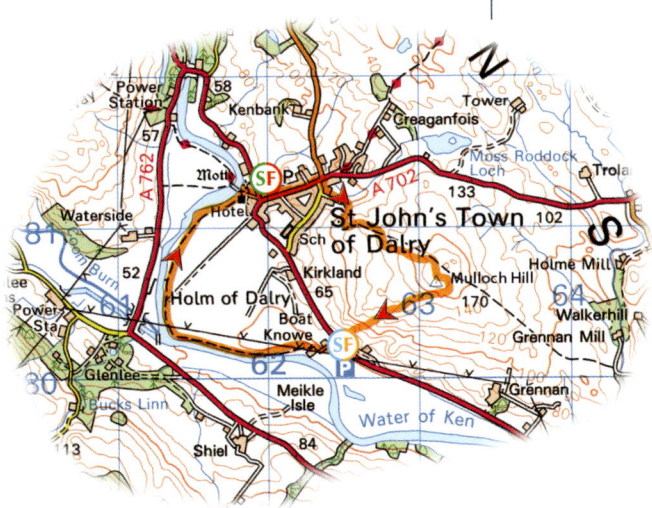

West flank of Mulloch Hill

Head directly uphill through the village. As the street gets less steep and bends right, turn sharp right in Kirkland Street, still gently uphill. In 50 metres, turn left at a footpath sign for Mulloch Hill and head up a walled lane to its end. Go through the kissing gate beside a field gate onto a track slanting up to the right.

The track goes through another field gate, this one with an inset walkers' gate. ◄ Then it bends left, directly uphill. After a short rise it bends right, with a wall to its left. At a crossing wall, the track goes through another gate. Now fork up left to another gate, again with inset walkers' gate. Bear right, as waymarked, slanting away from the wall across open field towards the highest point ahead. The fence crossing ahead has a gate not seen as you approach as it's behind a hump of the hill. Through this gate, bear right, waymarked, heading south to the cairn and trig point summit of **Mulloch Hill**.

Every field gate on the ascent has such an inset walkers' gate, so any gate without one is off-route.

Ignore a faint path heading off left (east). ◄ Keep on south down to a nearby wall. Turn down to the right beside the wall to the field corner. Here, take a gate on the left then one on the right to continue downhill, now to the left of the wall. After 300 metres, a gate in the wall lets you through to continue downhill once again to its right.

This path heads towards Balmaclellan.

With the main road seen below, and gorse bushes beside the wall, bear right on a visible path to the left of a small stream. Keep down left of the stream to a kissing gate under small trees to the **A713** main road. ◄

A lay-by on the left is the alternative start/end point.

ROUTE 23 – MULLOCH HILL

Go straight across into a track signed for **Boat Knowe**. Just before this house, turn right at a wooden signpost for Dalry. A grass track leads to a gate, then along the top of the flood banking, soon alongside the **Water of Ken**. There's also a rougher path nearer the river. Riverside trees are good (as they drop stuff into the water for the fish and provide shade for our scaly friends) and bad (as they block our views of the river).

As the river bends right (north) you hear and glimpse the tail race of Glenlee Power Station. The paths rejoin to run through scrub to the edge of **Dalry**. Pass below the churchyard to the end of the long wooden footbridge. Turn up right, away from the footbridge. ▶ Keep up ahead to the foot of the Main Street.

> Steps on your right lead into the churchyard, where there's a Covenanter grave in the corner down right.

THE COVENANTERS AT DALRY

In November 1666, four soldiers set upon an old man in Dalry, demanding the fines due for his non-attendance at the Episcopal church services so repugnant to his Presbyterian beliefs. (Instead he will have been attending informal conventicles led by an ousted former minister out in the hills.)

When the soldiers proposed to torture the old man – purely for the fun of it, as he had no money – a Covenanter who happened to be in the Clachan Inn shot one of them through the body with a pistol loaded with pieces of an old clay pipe.

Dalry Church and Covenanter tomb

This was the start of an armed rebellion, a march on Edinburgh by 900 lightly armed Covenanters. At Rullion Green in the Pentland Hills, they were met and defeated by a much larger force of professional soldiers. The rebellion marks the start of the persecutions of the Killing Times (see Introduction).

ROUTE 24
Waterside Hill

Start/finish	St John's Town of Dalry, Clachan Inn (NX 619 812)
Distance	7km (4½ miles)
Ascent	200m (700ft)
Harshness	2
Approx time	2hr 15min
Terrain	Paths, and 1.5km of quiet road
Highest point	Waterside Hill, 172m
Parking	Street parking in Dalry
Variants	This walk is even better when combined with Dunveoch Hill (Route 25) for two delightful little hills: 12km (7½ miles) of distance, and 350m (1100ft) ascent – about 3hr 30min

For Southern Upland Way walkers, Waterside Hill may come as a relief after several miles of harsh track and tarmac; or possibly not, as the steepish ascent comes at the end of a very long day indeed from Bargrennan right through the Galloway Hills. But that ascent is very short: just 80m of height gain. The path is grassy and good, and the summit is graced with some rocky knolls and a wide view along the Glenkens valley.

For those who haven't previously tramped the tracks all the way from Bargrennan, the only downside is the small but nasty swamp crossed at the base of the hill. That, and the insistent urge to turn left at Glenlee Bridge and add in the slightly bigger and even better Dunveoch Hill. The swamp path was helpfully repaired in 2019. But the urges to also do Dunveoch – best just give in to those.

Take the alley to the right of Clachan Inn, with a Southern Upland Way (SUW) signpost hidden in a tree. It becomes a path down to a fine suspension bridge over **Water of Ken**. Cross and turn down left into a riverside path.

The path runs in scrubby woodland, out of sight of the river. Fork left, to avoid leaving the woodland. The various paths arrive at a wide pool of the river and continue beside it. At 800 metres from the footbridge, bear right through a gateway then turn left to continue along the raised flood banking.

The flood bank and path bend back to the right, to the **A762**. Turn left to cross **Coom Burn**, then right in a small path through tangled woods. The

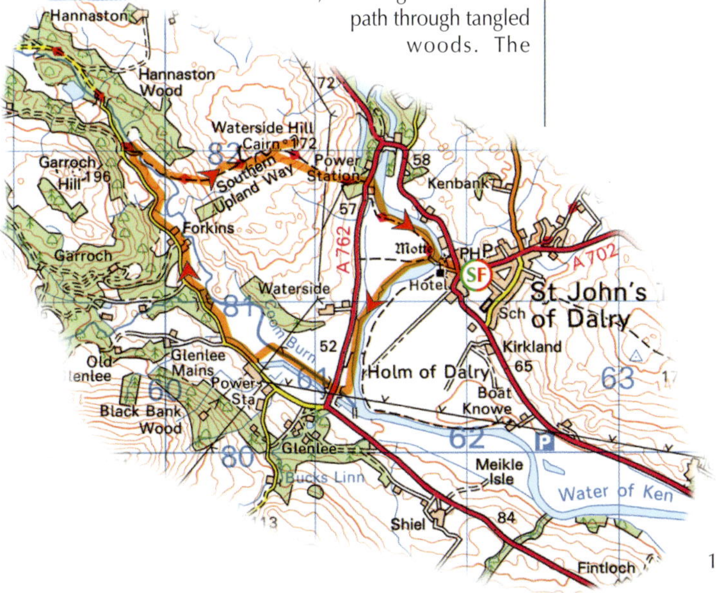

Footbridge over Water of Ken, with Dalry Church

141

To include Dunveoch Hill, you'll turn left just before the bridge – see Route 25.

path emerges to open field alongside Coom Burn, and passes under power lines, with **Glenlee Power Station** seen on the left. Pass through a fallen fence and at once turn down left to a small gate. Follow the left edge of a field then a path through blackthorn scrub to arrive on the small Glenlee road.

Turn right for 500 metres to Glenlee Bridge (which crosses Glenlee Burn, a side stream, rather than the main Garroch Burn). ◄ In another 1.2km along the lane, look out for a SUW signpost marking an earth path down to the right. The path runs alongside Garroch Burn to a footbridge. Across this, turn downstream, on a damp path that soon passes through a small swamp. Thankfully, the path's now been inproved to allow dry-foot passage in most conditions. Soon a gate leads out onto the foot of Waterside Hill.

A clear path winds up through bracken to the hill top, which has rocky knolls. At the highest point of the path, there's a sudden view down to Dalry. Here, leave the path and cross three of the rocky knolls to reach the cairned summit of **Waterside Hill**.

Return just south of west – the compass bearing may be needed, as the rock knolls are confusing. Rejoin the path and follow it down through bracken to reach a gate to the left of a wood and to the right of a white-painted **power station**. A stony path leads down beside the power station's fish ladder to the **A762**.

Rhinns of Kells seen from Waterside Hill

Turn right for 50 metres, and cross to a small gate. The path leads to riverside fields. Follow **Water of Ken** downstream to the footbridge at the walk start.

ROUTE 25
Dunveoch

Start/finish	Glenlee lane (NX 601 813)
Distance	7.5km (5 miles)
Ascent	200m (700ft)
Harshness	3
Approx time	2hr 15min (plus scrambling)
Terrain	Tracks, a field edge, and a slightly rugged hill
Highest point	Dunveoch Hill, 258m
Parking	Verge parking on east side of the lane near Garroch Sawmill (Forkins on OS map)
Variants	For a really gentle walk, a track bypasses Dunveoch Hill. Or combine with Waterside Hill – see Route 24.

Dunveoch Hill is a mountain in miniature – bristling with bare rock, even if much of it is at a near-horizontal angle. Who would have expected scrambling opportunities on something so gently sloping and only 258m tall? And the approaches are equally rewarding, by streamside and well-managed old woodland and a spacious open moorland. Even better, if time allows, is to combine the hill with an even smaller one, Waterside Hill (Route 24), and so extend the approach route back all the way to Dalry.

Head south down the lane to cross Glenlee Bridge (which crosses Glenlee Burn, a side stream, rather than the main Garroch Burn). ▶ Just after the bridge, a small gate on the right leads to a duckboard and a streamside path. Ignore a dangerous old bridge over the stream; just beyond it, the path ends at a small gate into a field corner with a micro-hydro turbine house.

Continue beside the stream then bear up left to a field gate at the furthest corner of the field. It leads onto a gravel track. Turn right, uphill, at once keeping ahead in a fainter track. This runs up into fields, and ends at a field gate. Keep uphill to the right of a small stream, to stone-walled

If approaching from Dalry, you'll be coming north up the lane and turning left just before the bridge.

sheep-handling pens. Pass to the right of these, and descend alongside a plantation to **Glenlee Burn**.

At the field foot, a small gate leads to a stout footbridge alongside the supply pipe for the micro-hydro scheme. A faint track heads upstream, then bends up to the right to join the rather clearer track that runs around the base of **Dunveoch Hill**. Follow this to the left until it emerges through a gate between fence (left) and wall (right) onto the open slopes of Dunveoch Hill.

To bypass Dunveoch Hill

It's hard to imagine anyone not consumed by a need to confront the rather rocky slope of this small hill. But such a person could simply stay on the track as it runs above Glenlee Burn then bends up right to pass through the wide, shallow pass west of Dunveoch Hill.

To ascend, head uphill, zigzagging on rough grass or, more easily, on opposite zigzags so as to link together the gentle rock slabs.

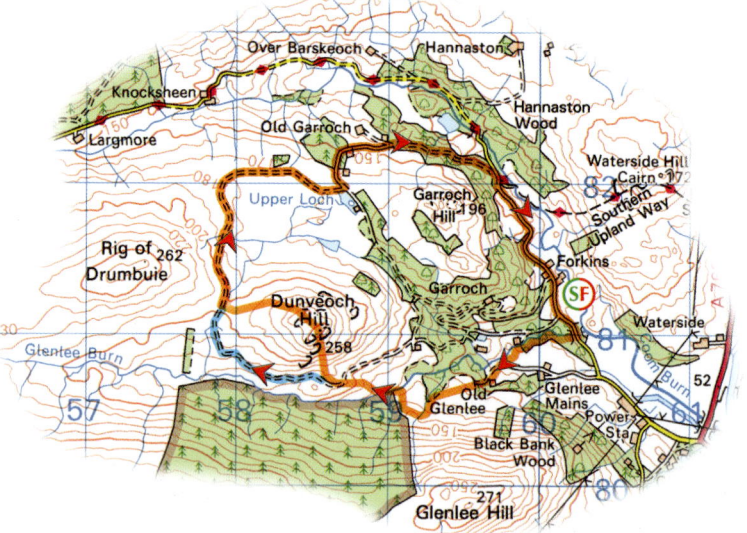

Dunveoch scrambling

Occasional steeper moments can be found by those who want to scramble. In particular, the final low rock wall below the summit can easily be walked round on the left, but its good hornfels rock has grippy handholds for all but the seriously scramble-averse.

From the summit of **Dunveoch Hill**, head northwest across a former fence to a sub-summit, then descend roughly west to rejoin the track as it crosses the wide, shallow pass to the west of the hill. The track runs across Garroch Moss, north then bending east. After 2km you meet a wider track beside the tree-girt **Upper Loch**. Turn back sharp left. The new track bends right twice, to run generally east. Ignore side tracks. After passing near **Old Garroch**, the track runs down in Long Wood, with imposing tall trees of ash, beech and oak, to arrive at the Glenlee lane. ▸

Keep ahead down the lane for 700 metres to close off the walk.

To continue over Waterside Hill, turn left for just 50 metres, and look out for a Southern Upland Way signpost on the right – now following Route 24.

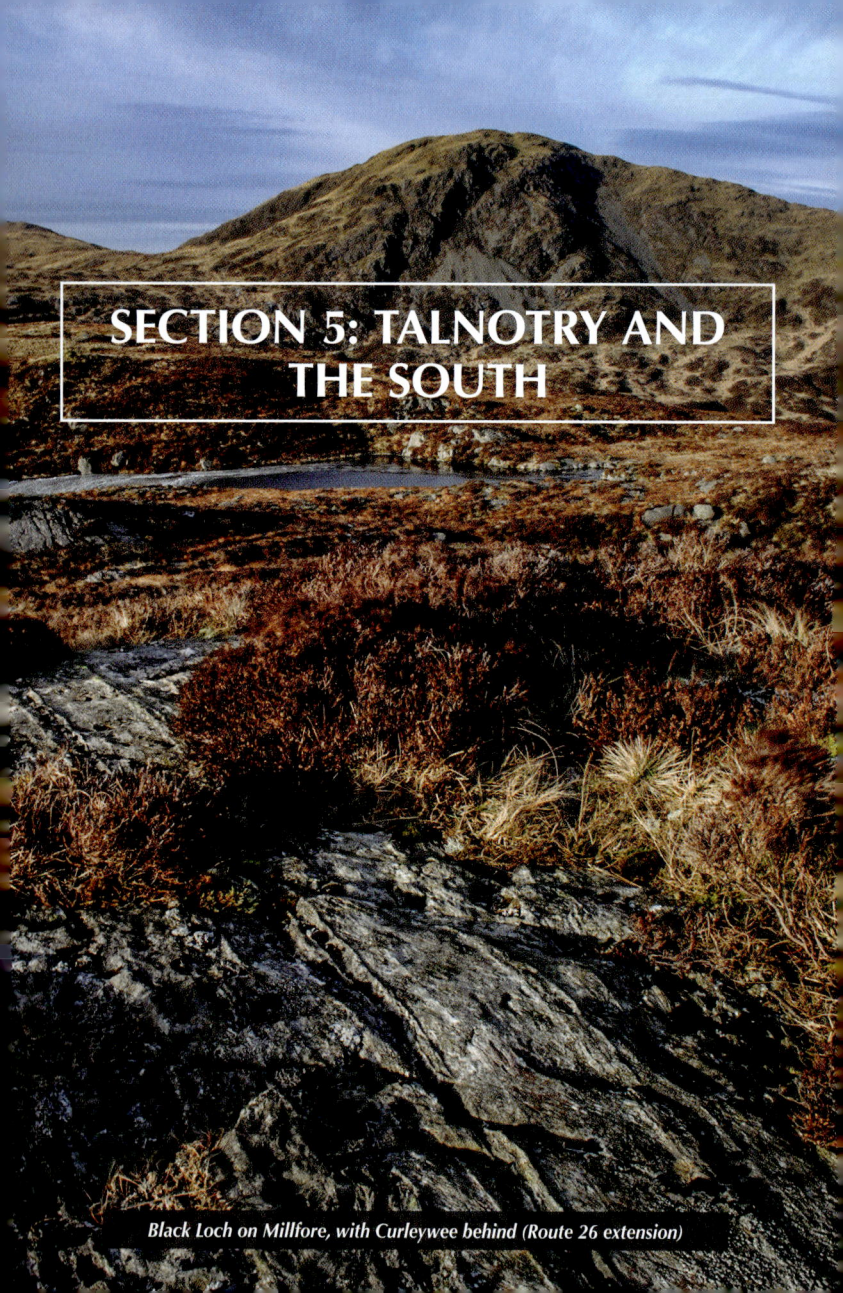

SECTION 5: TALNOTRY AND THE SOUTH

Black Loch on Millfore, with Curleywee behind (Route 26 extension)

INTRODUCTION

An ancient pilgrim path and drove road cuts across the Galloway Hills, separating off Cairnsmore of Fleet from the hills to the north. Tarmacked as the A712, the dividing road has been romantically renamed as the Queen's Way – Mary Queen of Scots was one of those early pilgrims to the shrine of St Ninian at Whithorn. The remote and rather bendy road, linking Dalry with Newton Stewart, runs past the wide waters of Clatteringshaws reservoir – perhaps the area's least interesting loch because of the way the hills lie back away from it. The road continues through plantations and across bouldery moorland, flanked on the south by the rocky slopes of Cairnsmore of Dee and Cairnsmore of Fleet, and by the largely forested lower slopes of the Minnigaff range to the north.

Midway along the road, Talnotry (no facilities or even roofed habitations) is an oasis of interestingness, with the spire of Murray's Monument on its little hill beside the rugged micro-mountain designated as a wild goat park, where the goats can usually be spotted as they are fed here through the winter. There are also some fine waterfalls and even a couple of sculptural artworks, reached by short walks (see Route 28). This is an access point for Millfore to the north (Route 28), although it's the side road to Auchenleck that offers the better access to the Minnigaffs range, including a full traverse (the extended version of Route 26).

A track bridge at Talnotry also opens up the rugged granite plateau of Cairnsmore of Fleet at its most interesting end. While all three of the area's Cairnsmores are big granite lumps, it's this end of this particular Cairnsmore (Route 29) that offers the bare rock slabs on top, the little lochans and the bewildering maze of bog grasses and peat.

Newton Stewart itself, the main gateway town to the Galloway Hills, gives a southerly and much gentler route onto Cairnsmore, reducing it to a grassy slope with a grand sea view (Route 30). Meanwhile, the ancient Wood of Cree, scraps of the original oaks that covered the lower ground around the hills, offers a couple of the shorter low-level walks that the rugged Galloways are otherwise somewhat short of. The final routes, 32 to 34, offer woodland and moorland, ancient chambered cairns and standing stones, a ruined castle and some ornamental waterfalls.

WALKING THE GALLOWAY HILLS

ROUTE 26
Larg Hill to Curleywee

Start/finish	Bridge near Auchenleck (NX 447 705)
Distance	19km (12 miles)
Ascent	850m (2800ft)
Harshness	3
Approx time	6hr 45min
Terrain	Forest roads, grassy ridges, and valley path, with rough ascent onto Sheuchanower and steep descent off Curleywee
Highest point	Lamachan Hill, 717m
Parking	Parking area at start of Forestry Commission track
Variants	For an easier but slightly longer descent off Curleywee, see Route 27. Extension over Millfore: 21km (13 miles) with 1100m (3700ft) ascent – about 8hr.

The Minnigaff Hills may be small, but they're as shaggy and wild as the mountain goats that roam over them. The approach from the south is defended by plantations. But the forest trudge is rewarded by a natural horseshoe route that includes Larg Hill.

Larg is gently grassy – it'll mislead you into thinking the walk ahead will be an easy one. Lamachan, too, is grassy, but leads into a knobbly ridgeline, excitingly bypassed by a path across the top of the northern slope. That path is narrow and slightly rocky, and was made in the first place by goats.

Curleywee is just as nice as its name. Weave up among scree and small crags to the grassy hollow at its top. The route threads down among more small crags onto a moorland of orange grasses and a dozen sky-coloured lochans. And for the valley descent there's a forgotten old path and a grassy riverbank.

Take the forest road running northwest. After 1km it runs alongside **Penkiln Burn**. In another 2km the ground up left has young trees (planted early 2010s), and views open ahead to show Larg Hill. The track crosses a first small concrete bridge, and 500 metres later it crosses a second one and is about to re-enter trees.

ROUTE 26 – LARG HILL TO CURLEYWEE

Turn up left, alongside the tree edge and Benroach Burn. After 300 metres, the right-hand (north) bank is obstructed by wind-blown trees. Cross to the awkward rough ground on the left side of the stream. Just above, a clear ride (tree gap) continues uphill, east. (The ride separates mid-sized trees on the right from the newly planted ones on the left.)

The ride arrives at the wall at the plantation top, south of Sheuchanower (400m contour ring). Turn north, with the wall on your right, across Sheuchanower's slight rise, then up the grassy slope and along the shoulder **Sheuchan Craig** to **Larg Hill**. At a wall junction, keep ahead to the summit cairn.

Head northeast, to the left of another wall, down to Nick of the Brushy. ▶ A small path leads up **Lamachan Hill**. The summit is marked by a gateway gap in a falling stone wall.

Head roughly northeast across the plateau, following occasional old iron fence posts, to **Bennanbrack**. Now descend southeast on a lumpy ridge. At 400 metres down the ridge, look out for the small goat path just down on the left; it takes an exciting line just below the ridge crest.

After Nick of Corners Gale, the goat path contours across the north side of a hump called Milldown to arrive in **Nick of Curleywee**. ▶ Go through a wall gap and head up the steep face of **Curleywee**.

Descend Curleywee with care. Head southeast across a slight col, over the spur top of Gaharn, and gently

The sharp dip is a small meltwater channel, from when ice filled the Loch Trool valley on your left. That same glacier has dumped granite boulders along the ridge.

For a note on geology, see Route 9.

Larg Hill from the slopes of Lamachan

WALKING THE GALLOWAY HILLS

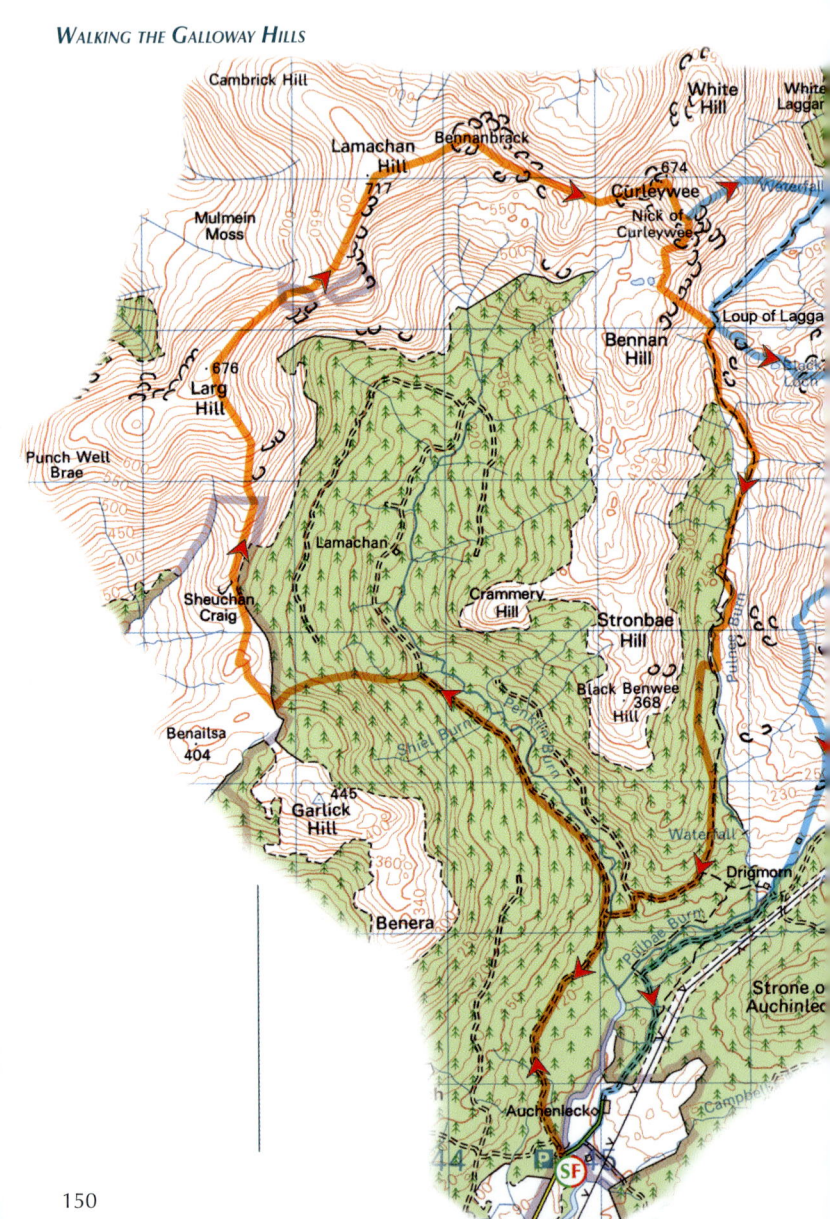

150

ROUTE 26 – LARG HILL TO CURLEYWEE

down for another 50 metres or so to the end of the level shoulder. ▶ Now turn down right to descend slightly west of south, weaving between rocky bits, onto a flat moorland. Cross this towards **Bennan Hill** to find a falling stone wall. Turn left down this, with a path. Keep downhill through a fence gate to **Loup of Laggan** pass.

The main route now turns to the right, down into the valley of **Pulnee Burn** then up right onto a forest track; refer to Route 27 for this final part of the walk, which returns you to **Auchenleck** and the walk start. Meanwhile, the truly energetic can continue ahead over Millfore.

For a longer but easier descent, switch now to Route 27 and follow it back to the walk start.

Continuation over Millfore

The horseshoe of the Minnigaff Hills can be extended over Millfore. The ascent, by the Black and White Lochs of Drigmorn, is rougher and wilder even than Curleywee; but once on the summit ridge, the going is gentler for the descent to Drigmorn and a short forest road finish.

From Loup of Laggan head directly uphill, east, on rugged ground to find **Black Loch** and then the larger **White Lochan**. The going now becomes grassy. Keep southeast along the ridgeline, then at the final slope head up east to the summit ridge and turn left to **Millfore** trig point.

Return southwest along the summit ridge and down the ridgeline beyond, passing the tiny lochan called Fuffock for the slight rise over **Drigmorn Hill**. Keep down southwest until the ridge steepens. Now turn left (south) down a steeper slope and then rough pastures to a gateway in a wall and the ruin of **Drigmorn**. The track beyond crosses Green Burn to a gravelled forest road. Turn right for 2km to **Auchenleck**, with the tarmac road leading ahead to the walk start.

Lamachan Hill from White Hill of Curleywee

ROUTE 27
Curleywee by Stronbae Hill

Start/finish	Bridge near Auchenleck (NX 447 705)
Distance	17km (10½ miles)
Ascent	700m (2300ft)
Harshness	4
Approx time	5hr 45min
Terrain	Forest roads, rough moorland of coarse grass and short heather, valley path for the descent
Highest point	Curleywee, 674m
Parking	Parking area at start of Forestry Commission track
Variants	The route could be extended to take in Millfore: see end of Route 26

Curleywee is the craggy one in Galloway's outer rim. With its pointy little summit and rocky lumps, Curleywee is crucial. So just in case you don't have time for the full Route 26, here's a shorter way up it.

The approach is pathless moorland, rather rough going, with one or two tiny hidden pools. It's the kind of place where you might come across Galloway's wild goats, or even the small herd of red deer. The less likely wildlife sighting would be a fellow human being.

Take the wide, smooth track northwards, in 200 metres keeping ahead as the main track bends left. After 1.5km, the **Penkiln Burn** is heard to the right of the track; at a track junction, turn right over the burn.

The track climbs gradually – ignore a side track on the left (which gives a view of Larg Hill). After about 1km the track dips to a wide turning area and crosses a stream. Then it rises, emerging into ground clear-felled for replanting in the late 2010s. Just 250 metres after the turning area, and before the track levels off, look out for a strip of willow above the track; on the right, here, a small incised stream runs down from the track. Here, head up (small cairn) for 20 metres, through the willows, to find the remains of a much older track.

Missed the turn-off point?

If you fail to spot the old track, continue on the new one until its end. It runs closer to Pulnee Burn than the old one marked on some maps. At the track end, turn up a gap in plantations, to meet the end of the northern branch of the older track at the top of the plantations. Keep uphill alongside a fallen wall, along the foot of a low crag, to reach the ridgeline north of **Black Benwee Hill**.

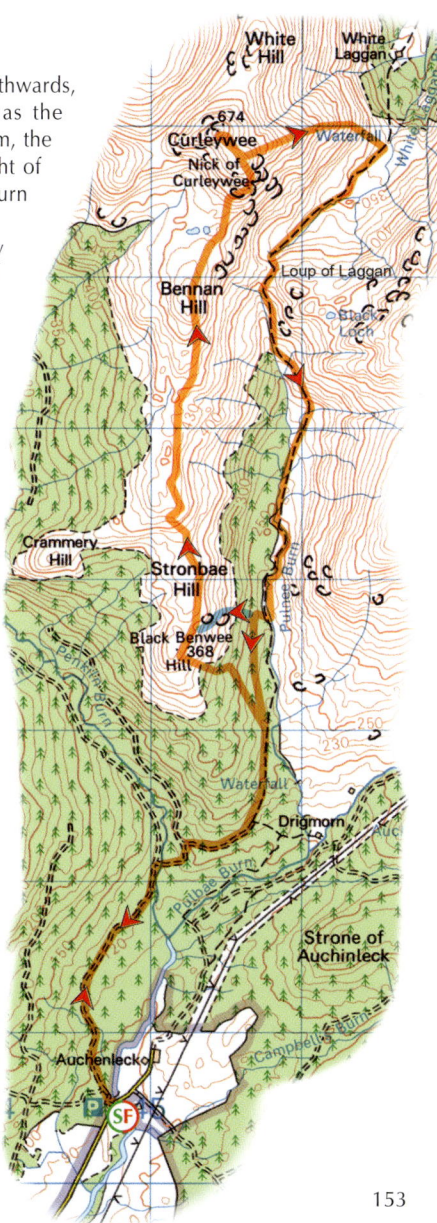

Curleywee from the south

Follow the old track to the right, rising along a higher line above the newer, smoother, wider one. After 400 metres, turn left onto a side track uphill. This zigzags, damp and faint, then turns directly up to the top edge of the plantations, emerging through a gap in clear-fell. Keep uphill to the cairn on **Black Benwee Hill**.

Turn north along the wide moorland ridge. The going is quite tough, on coarse grass and low heather, although intermittent traces of paths can be found. ◄ Just north of Black Benwee Hill you cross a broken wall, then there's a gentle rise to the level section over **Stronbae Hill**. The next minor hump is White Benwee Hill – the name 'White' correctly implies the going is becoming a bit grassier and a bit less heathery. A small pool lies at the foot of the more serious ascent to **Bennan Hill**, which has a cairn on top. Now you drop slightly, cross a broken wall, and confront the rugged slopes of Curleywee itself.

There are fine views back to the Cree estuary, and sideways to Larg and Lamachan westwards, and Millfore the other way.

The slope ahead is quite craggy. The key is to aim directly across the highest point of the wide saddle for the closest point of the slope. Then slant up to the right, to arrive on the southeastern outlier called Gaharn. It turns out to be a shoulder rather than a sub-summit. Head along the level shoulder northwest for the short rise to **Curleywee** summit, with cairn.

Return over the spur top of Gaharn, and gently down for another 50 metres or so to the end of the level shoulder. Now descend a grassy spurline northeast. As it steepens, turn down directly east, seeking out the slightly higher lines rather than the grassy hollows. At the slope foot, keeping well to the left of a fenceline, cross seriously tussocky ground to reach a path. ◄

White Laggan bothy is 500 metres to the left down this path.

Route 27 – Curleywee by Stronbae Hill

Turn right along the path, which crosses through a fence with a stile. It runs very attractively along the upper valley, before the slight rise to the pass, the **Loup of Laggan**. ▶ The path continues quite steeply down beyond, running to the left of the stream. After passing the top corner of plantations, the path moves left, away from the stream, crossing a side stream at the level valley floor to reach a ruined sheepfold.

From this point on, the old path fades away. Join the **Pulnee Burn** and follow its left bank, where the grass is shorter and the ground is well drained on the whole. After 800 metres downstream there's a corner of the plantations, with the stream bending across the valley leftwards. Here, you can cross the stream and stay on its pleasantly grassy right bank. At the next plantation corner, the old path line has a gateway but that leads only to a mess of fallen trees, so edge round between the stream and the forest wall, then recross the stream if you wish.

In another 250 metres, you're opposite the end of a forest road up on your right. ▶ Recross the stream at the point where the fallen wall opposite is replaced by fencing. Cross the fencing, head up through a gap in plantations (in 2018 this was clear-fell to the left, tall trees ready for felling on the right) and head up for 100 metres to join the end of the wide, smooth new forest road.

Turn left, following the track south above the stream and rejoining the outward route to cross **Penkiln Burn** and then turn left to the road at **Auchenleck** and the walk start.

At the top of the pass you could turn up left to take in Millfore – see Route 26.

Some 150 metres downstream ahead, the wall switches to the left side of the stream.

Loup of Laggan pass

ROUTE 28
Millfore

Start/finish	Murray's Monument, A712 (NX 490 720)
Distance	12km (7½ miles)
Ascent	650m (2100ft)
Harshness	4
Approx time	4hr 30min
Terrain	Tracks, paths, and grassy summit; but a tough ascent between trees and over Fell of Talnotry
Highest point	Millfore, 656m
Parking	Grey Mare's Tail car park below and just east of Murray's Monument
Variants	Murray's Monument short walk: 3km (2 miles) with 150m (500ft) ascent – about 1hr

Millfore is a grassy and comfortable summit, ideal for lounging in the sunshine and peering northwards at the full sweep of the Galloway Hills. The southwards approach gives a convenient hill day, with moorland of slightly rocky grass, three waterfalls and a couple of sculptures. However, there's a sting in the beginning: the make-the-best-of-it ascent through plantations and then the rough heathery plantlife of Fell of Talnotry. Note that further felling will be happening around 2020, which may complicate the route-finding here.

To enjoy the waterfalls without the hillwalking, there's the Forestry Commission's short waymarked walk at Murray's Monument.

Begin by taking the very short path upstream to look at the waterfall, mapped as Buck Loup but labelled by the Forestry Commission as Grey Mare's Tail. It is visible from the car park. A low wall blocks the path end but it's easy to continue around it for a closer view. Retrace your steps.

Take the path uphill past an info board towards **Murray's Monument**. About halfway up to the monument, there's a waymark post and a fainter side path on the right. But for now, continue up ahead, with the path crossing some bare rock on the way to the tall stone column.

ROUTE 28 – MILLFORE

ALEXANDER MURRAY

Murray was born in 1775, the son of a shepherd and labourer, in Dunkitterick Cottage, whose ruins lie 2km east of the monument on the old smugglers' route to Gatehouse of Fleet. He had only a year of formal education, weak health, and eyesight so poor he couldn't even find the cows, never mind the sheep on the shaggy side of Cairnsmore. Accordingly he became a self-taught linguist with whatever scraps of books and papers he could pick up. It looks like the passing smugglers dropped their fish-and-chips wrappers in French, Latin, German, Hebrew, and even Arabic, Abyssinian, Anglo-Saxon, Lappish and Welsh.

Murray eventually became professor of oriental languages at Edinburgh University. He is not credited with the fundamental discovery that almost all European languages are descended from a now-lost common Indo-European root. That's because his death at the age of 37 from tuberculosis prevented the publication of his insight before two Germans found it independently, a couple of years later. His monument was built in 1835, through the 'exertions and skill' of Stewart of Cairnsmore house (passed on Route 30).

Return down over the little rock step and turn left on the fainter path that you passed on the way up. It passes behind the monument's knoll to meet a wider uphill path (which is also used by mountain bikes as part of the 7stanes network, so watch out). Turn right up it to reach a forest road.

The tree gap above has become overgrown. So turn right for 200 metres to the start of clear-fell above the track. ▶ Turn up sharp left on a steep wheelmarked track. It zigzags up the clear-felled zone, then slants gently up left to the clear-fell's top left corner. Straight up ahead is a slight dip with a stream in it and a tree gap. Head up this gap, on rough grass going, getting less bad. The gap slants just west of north to reach the top of the trees.

For the short Murray's Monument walk, keep ahead along this track to where it crosses the Grey Mare's Tail Burn and rejoins the main route.

Millfore from Stronbae Hill

If you care, the actual high point is 200 metres further north.

Head up north, in rather deep grass and heather, which soon eases as you approach the cairn on **Fell of Talnotry**. ◄ Now head northwest, down over a broken wall and a fence. Pass under high power lines and cross the dip called Nick of Slannyvenach to rise up slightly rocky grass moorland towards **Drigmorn Hill**, the southwest ridge of Millfore. In clear conditions, the Black Cairn at Fuffock can be seen on the skyline. Heading up northwest will bring you to the ridgeline at or near this **cairn**, with the tiny outlet trickle of the pool called Fuffock just behind.

The name is from Gaelic Meall Fuar, cold hill.

Head up the gentle grassy ridgeline to Millfore's southwest top, cairned. A grassy, near-level ridge leads on to the trig point at the main summit of **Millfore**. ◄

Head down the wide, grassy flank southeast. The hill shoulder called **Kirkloch** has some rocky outcrops on the right, so if you come to crags facing south, head a bit further left. A steeper drop (which could be bypassed on the left) leads down to a dip with a fence. Cross a final short rise, with a little path possibly to be found, to reach a smooth gravel track.

Follow this down to the right, into broken forestry plantations.

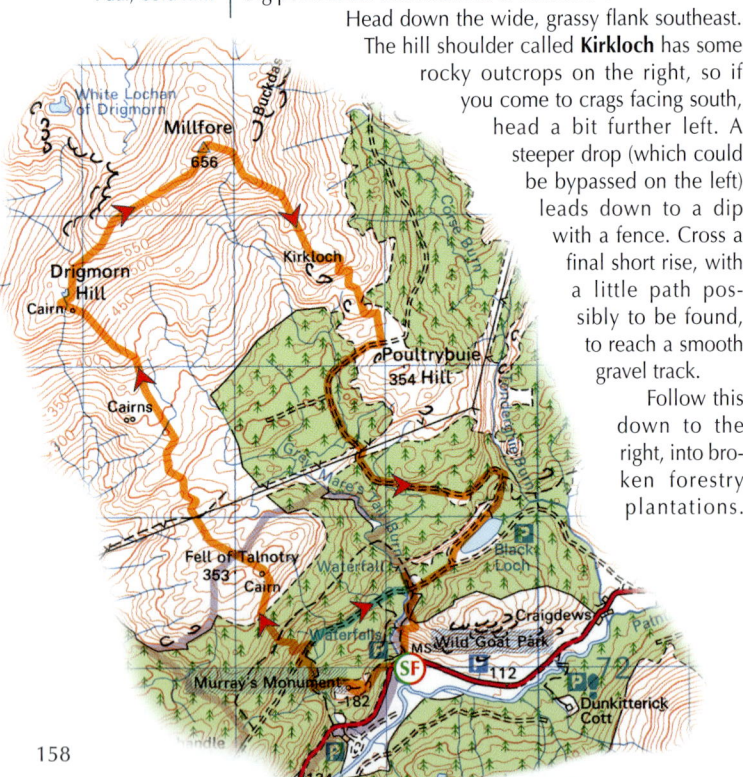

Route 28 – Millfore

Ignore a side track on the right. Pass under the high power lines; then the track slants down leftwards, east. Above Tonderghie Burn (heard rather than seen) it turns downhill, then bends back right to run above the **Black Loch**. A tall sculpture, called *Eye* (by Colin Rose), is below the track at the loch head.

The top of Murray's Monument is now seen through the pass ahead. Turn right at a track junction. In 400 metres, the track has a culvert over **Grey Mare's Tail Burn**. ▶ Just before this, a waymark post marks the path turning down left. But first, take a rough path the other way, upstream to the right of the burn, to visit the Grey Mare's Tail waterfall. Return, and cross the track onto a good grassy path. It passes through a drystone-walled enclosure, where there are a couple of granite lumps carved by Matt Baker as the *Quorum* sculpture. ▶

The path runs down to left of the stream, then climbs slightly to the left. As it descends towards the car park, at a left-hand bend, a small bracken path on the right leads down to another waterfall, the Foot Loup. Return to the main path and follow it down to the A712, with the **car park** across the stream on your right.

The short Murray's Monument walk comes in here.

There were originally three blocks; you can try and find the one that's fallen out of the wall.

The Eye sculpture at Black Loch

WALKING THE GALLOWAY HILLS

ROUTE 29
Cairnsmore of Fleet from the north

Start/finish	Murray's Monument, A712 (NX 487 716)
Distance	14.5km (9 miles)
Ascent	800m (2700ft)
Harshness	5
Approx time	6hr
Terrain	Rugged slopes and moorland of heather, grass and granite lumps, with grassy going over Meikle Mulltaggart and a forest track to finish
Highest point	Cairnsmore of Fleet, 711m
Parking	Two unsigned pull-offs on north side of A712 below and west of Murray's Monument (not the Grey Mare's Tail car park 600 metres east)

The southern Route 30 presents Cairnsmore of Fleet as a large, grassy hill with a good path and a great view. The northern end seems like a different hill completely. It's the wild moorland south of Craignelder that justifies the designation of this National Nature Reserve as a 'high-level granite bog of international importance'.

This is a place of tiny pools and bare granite slabs. In mist, it's deeply mysterious. But a clear day is better as it lets you find the little Coo Lochans and the scenically placed Brockloch Cairn. The going is rugged, at least until you approach Meikle Mulltaggart. But, with all respect to Scottish Natural Heritage, it's not especially boggy.

Murray's Monument and Cairnsmore of Fleet

ROUTE 29 – CAIRNSMORE OF FLEET FROM THE NORTH

On the south side of the road, take the wide forest track marked 'no authorised vehicles'. It runs down with a former campsite field on its left to a bridge over a river. Clugie Linn waterfall is directly under the bridge and not seen. In another 100 metres, the track divides.

Turn left for 100 metres, then turn up to the right, beside a granite wall. Head up to the right of the wall, in very rough vegetation, with traces of a path. ▶ There are patchy plantations alongside the wall.

As the wall bends right, keep ahead through a gateway gap in it. Continue uphill, beside a decaying fence at first. Head uphill on grassy heather with bits of rock, on a rounded spurline with very steep ground around the corner on the right. Many of the rock slabs are easily angled and can be walked up, a relief from the rougher vegetation. The small path can still be found in places and the vegetation eases as height is gained.

At 550m level, a cairn stands on granite slabs. Now the going is very much pleasanter on bare rock and short grass and moss. Another rock-standing cairn is further up, before the small cairn on **Craignelder**.

When old-fashioned feet and inches are finally forgotten and the 610m contour line loses any 2000ft magic it may have had, you may feel that **Millfore Hill**, 300 metres away and a big 1m more in altitude, needs a visit. ▶ Head northeast over flat ground, passing to the left of a small pool, to find the cairn a few steps beyond the highest point, with good views northeast.

Return from Millfore Hill, passing to the left of the small pool and descending south. Arrive at the near-right (west) corner of the wide level moorland saddle, where there's an area of bare granite with squatting boulders and the **Brockloch Cairn**. From here, a couple of small cairns give vague directions southeast across the moorland to a broken stile at the high point of a crossing fence. The two tiny **Coo Lochans** are just beyond. Head south for about 500 metres, then bear southeast past some slightly less tiny pools onto an unnamed moorland hump (587m). The summit is unmarked.

> If this guidebook adds users to this route, the path will get considerably more helpful here.

> If not, just descend southeast from Craignelder.

WALKING THE GALLOWAY HILLS

> Meikle Mulltaggart is a mere 10m higher than Craignelder, which is surprising as it feels as though it's considerably above it.

From here, the going is more ordinary but also much gentler grassland without granite lumps. A quad-bike track leads southwest along the summit plateau for the short rise to **Meikle Mulltaggart**. Fencing marked on Explorer maps is long decayed away. The quad-bike track bypasses to the right of the summit of Meikle Mulltaggart, which despite its fine name (and despite topping the supposedly magical 2000ft/610.4m mark) lacks a summit cairn. ◀

Rejoin the quad-bike path, down into the well-marked saddle and up to a fence gate just beyond. The quad path leads on up **Cairnsmore**. As the slope eases, bear right, across grassland, with the large summit cairn soon appearing ahead. As well as the substantial cairn, there is a trig point, a ruined hut, and a monument to crashed aircraft (including one airship).

Head west, gently downhill, soon coming across a fine view-point **cairn** 300 metres from the summit.

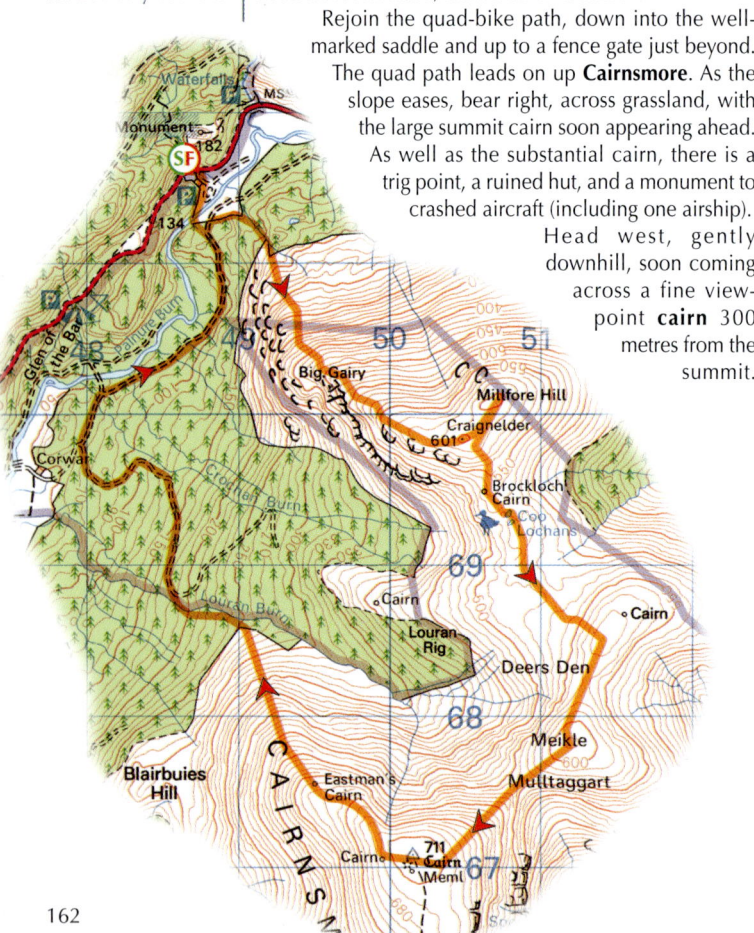

North end, Cairnsmore of Fleet

(This cairn is off the true ridgeline, and in mist it's better to take a direct line heading northwest for the more distant Eastman's Cairn.) Continue down northwest on a gentle wide spurline scattered with blocks of granite, to **Eastman's Cairn**, where the spurline steepens.

The slope here is convex, with the continuing spurline not visible below, so continue down carefully northwest to gain the spurline as it carries on below. The going gets rougher, with heather and occasional overgrown boulderfields, so it's with some relief that you arrive at the top of plantations. Aim to the bottom right corner of open hill, with trees on your right as well as ahead.

At this corner there's a stile over the fence at the plantation top. Just to the right is the fair-sized **Louran Burn**. Head downhill to the left of the burn, on a small path. After 400 metres, the burn dives into a narrow gorge with natural trees. Cross it just above this, and go down to the right of the deep little gorge. There's a fine little waterfall at the gorge top, difficult to see even in winter with the leaves off. ▶

The adventurous could get into the gorge at its foot and attempt to paddle upstream for a sight of the waterfall.

Just below the head of the gorge, you come to the corner of a wide, smooth forest road. Follow this gently downhill, away from the stream. There are some open views at first, as the track winds down to the valley floor near **Corwar**. At a track junction, follow the main track to the right. After 350 metres, and before the track's bridge

Coo Lochan, with Cairnsmore of Fleet

over **Palnure Burn**, take a side track on the right. This runs around the base of Craignelder, with ground above clear-felled (mid 2010s), to the track junction on the outward walk.

Turn left across the river back to the A712 below **Murray's Monument**.

BOG OF INTERNATIONAL IMPORTANCE

Cairnsmore has been described as a high-level granite bog of international importance: as such it is a National Nature Reserve. Hen harriers may still survive here, while peregrines and merlins are more likely sightings.

The plateau north of the summit is 'dwarf shrub heath', with heather, dwarf willow, sedges and moss. The summit itself, being drier, is grassy or short, wind-clipped heather. The peat is 7000 years old and down to 10m deep, and when healthy is growing at 1mm per year, second only to tropical rainforest as a natural form of carbon capture.

ROUTE 30

Cairnsmore of Fleet from the south

Start/finish	Cairnsmore Hill car park (NX 462 632)
Distance	15km (9½ miles)
Ascent	750m (2500ft)
Harshness	2
Approx time	5hr 15min
Terrain	Good hill path, grassy plateau, rough grassy descent and tracks
Highest point	Cairnsmore of Fleet, 711m
Parking	Turn off A75 at 800 metres east of Palnure. The minor road bends left, and goes between piers of a former rail bridge; parking is in a disused track on the right.

Cairnsmore of Fleet is the southernmost 2000ft summit in Scotland. Its isolated position above the Solway Firth explains its wide views, as well as the memorial to crashed aeroplanes at the summit. Cairnsmore is also a high-altitude bog; however, that bit lies to the north of the summit. This gentler route is on comfortable grass, with a rather mysterious old path (perhaps formed by peat cutters) zigzagging up the broad slope above the wide Cree valley.

After the pleasant plateau wander, the descent is rather more rugged, with some granite boulderfields to weave around. But at the slope foot, another old track leads conveniently across the moor back to Cairnsmore farm.

Head up the track and through a little iron gate onto the driveway to Cairnsmore farm. Keep ahead up this for 800 metres to the first buildings. Here, bear right on an estate track, then turn right at a small sign up a path through rhododendron and laurel. At a higher track, turn left, to reach the end of the track above **Cairnsmore farm**.

Take the gate ahead, and bear right up a field to a gate at its top left corner. A clear path runs uphill through plantations. At a junction, keep ahead, signposted for Cairnsmore summit.

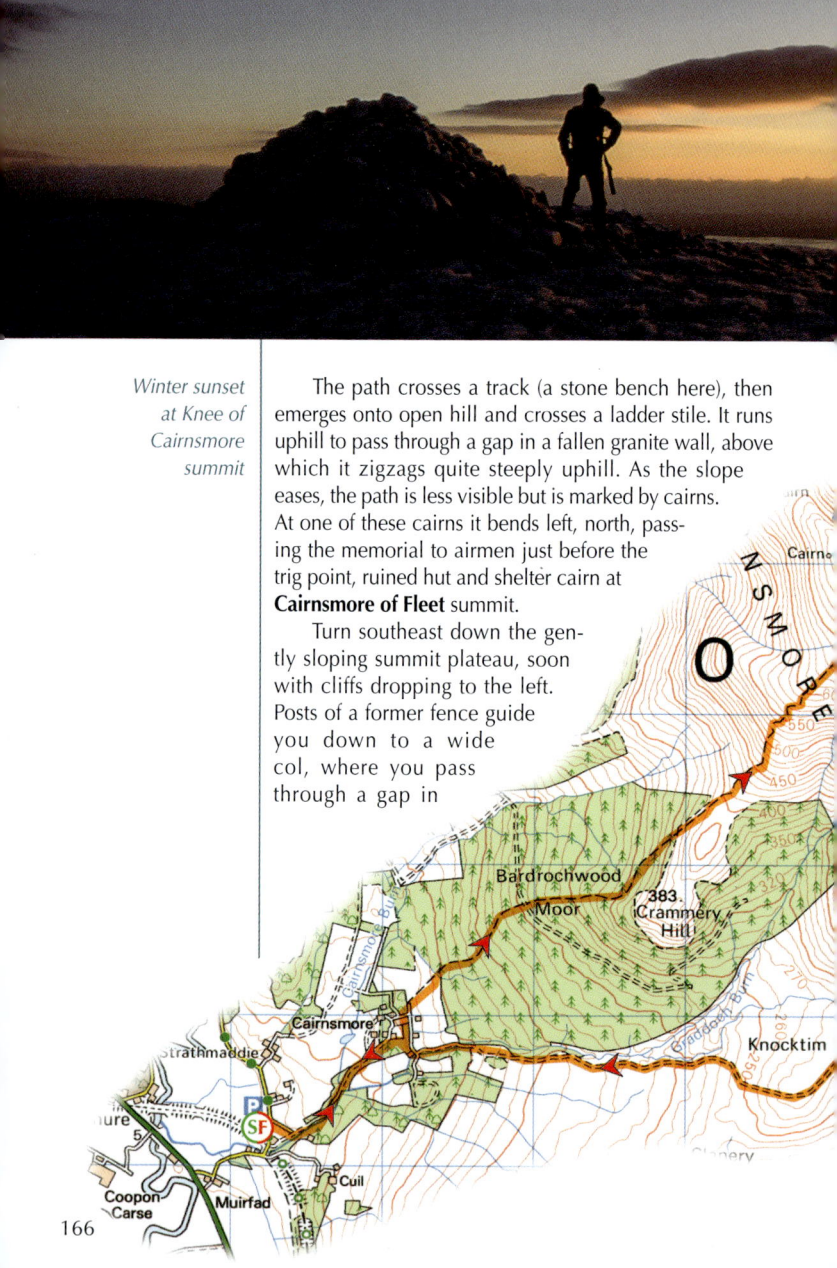

Winter sunset at Knee of Cairnsmore summit

The path crosses a track (a stone bench here), then emerges onto open hill and crosses a ladder stile. It runs uphill to pass through a gap in a fallen granite wall, above which it zigzags quite steeply uphill. As the slope eases, the path is less visible but is marked by cairns. At one of these cairns it bends left, north, passing the memorial to airmen just before the trig point, ruined hut and shelter cairn at **Cairnsmore of Fleet** summit.

Turn southeast down the gently sloping summit plateau, soon with cliffs dropping to the left. Posts of a former fence guide you down to a wide col, where you pass through a gap in

ROUTE 30 – CAIRNSMORE OF FLEET FROM THE SOUTH

an old wall. Head uphill, southeast, and at the top of the slope turn south across the level plateau to the large ancient cairn at its far end, marking the summit of **Knee of Cairnsmore**. ▶

This is Scotland's most southerly 2000ft top.

Descend grassy ground southwest on a vague spurline. As the ground steepens, find a grassy way down south between granite boulderfields. Cross the head of a shallow stream hollow onto the moorland beyond, named as **Knocktim**. Turn southwest along the crest of this on short moss and heather, after 400 metres or so joining a faint old track.

At the tip of Knocktim (NX 496 634) the track bends right, west. It runs down rough peaty pasture, becoming a stony farm track, and joining **Graddoch Burn**, with forest plantations opposite. The track runs down to a gate, where it fades into a field. Head down the right-hand edge next to the stream to another gate. Through this, the track continues down to the left of the stream, then across it at a bridge with a 5-ton weight limit. It continues downhill, now to the right of the stream, to a track T-junction near a house.

Turn right, and in about 150 metres turn down left in the laurel-wood path you arrived on, to return to the **car park**.

Approaching Cairnsmore of Fleet summit from the south

ROUTE 31
Clints of Dromore

Start/finish	Scottish Natural Heritage visitor centre at Dromore farm (NX 554 638)
Distance	13km (8 miles)
Ascent	400m (1300ft)
Harshness	4
Approx time	4hr 30min
Terrain	Granite lumps thinly covered with grass and heather; a mildly scrambly descent from 'Clint Eastward' can be bypassed; grassy going over Craig Hill
Highest point	Craig Hill, 357m
Parking	At visitor centre; toilets, unstaffed visitor centre
Variants	Shorter 'Mountain End Path', waymarked, and very short 'Inbye Path'

The Clints of Dromore have all the cragginess of Galloway's granite heartland in a convenient small package, just right for a half-day or one when the higher tops are shrouded in cloud. Note though that, while not high, it is tough going on the heathery moorland in back of the clints. The official Mountain End Path is soft and peaty, and stays back from the granity lumps; so our route takes a slightly higher line, with a moment of scrambly descent off the main clint.

For contrast, the second half of the walk leaves the granite for gentler grassy going over the misnamed Craig Hill – completely crag-free apart from some granite erratic boulders. The walk also includes a visitor centre with some indoor displays, and granite sculptures by Galloway artist Matt Baker.

Take the track continuing past the visitor centre car park, northeast towards the viaduct. After a cattle grid, fork off right to follow the bank of **Big Water of Fleet**. There's a small path along the riverbank and a wider grass track in the field alongside. After 400 metres, the river bends left, with a willow thicket on the opposite bank: here, a

ROUTE 31 – CLINTS OF DROMORE

midstream boulder has a bronze rake on a chain – this is *Scene Shifter*, the first of the sculptures by Matt Baker.

Take a path away from the river to rejoin the track and pass under the high **viaduct**. ▶ Continue ahead past a picnic area with info boards. After 200 metres, a signpost for the Inbye Path points back left on another track.

> Immediately, you could head up steeply left to shortcut to the railbed above.

> Just ahead, past the signpost, are the low humps and hummocks of **Little Cullendoch**, a former township settlement. A second Matt Baker sculpture (*Heart*) lurks among the stone walls there.

The signposted track rises gently to join the railbed on its embankment. You could turn back left along the embankment, to where a stile leads onto the viaduct, and then retrace your steps to follow the railbed southwest. ▶ The railbed track passes through a small cutting, with slabby greywacke rock. About 300 metres along the track, it passes through a second, gloomier cutting.

> The short, easy Inbye Path will stay on this former railway to pass above Dromore.

> High on the uphill wall, a cluster of slaty stones dangle from a chain: this is *Ocean*, the next **sculpture** by Matt Baker. Unlike the granite, these greywacke stones split to flat slabs, showing their bedding as ocean-bottom mud.

In another 200 metres, a signpost 'Mountain End Path' indicates a kissing gate on the right. The path starts on reinforced duckboard but immediately becomes a steep little path directly uphill through the gap between two granite clints. ▶ Emerging above the rocky knolls, bear up slightly right to a couple of symbolical 'cloud seats' (made by Ali Jeffries), made of resin and powdered rock.

Now a faint, damp path leads along the clints, with waymark posts well placed on skyline points. (The path runs mostly on the northward slope, a little back from the crestline, but this walk will mostly follow the more interesting crestline.) Follow the small path northwest gently uphill, then bending west and climbing more steeply. As the moorland plateau levels off, continue on the

> The granite here has visible crystals and is very different from the greywacke in the railway cuttings.

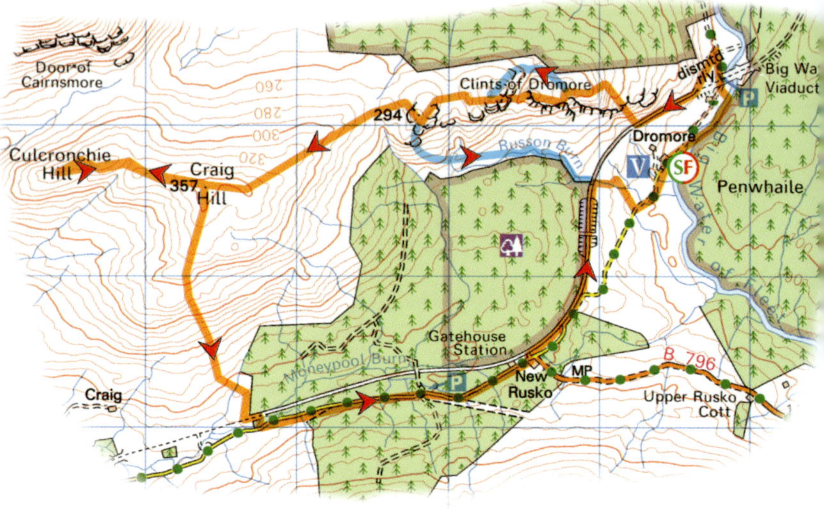

WALKING THE GALLOWAY HILLS

Cloud seat, Clints of Dromore

path for 250 metres, passing the head of a little valley between the clints. Then leave the path to the headland just beyond the little valley, where a rock knob has what looks like a small, low cairn. This is in fact *Hush*, another sculpture by Matt Baker (NX 5475 6415): a cluster of small, chained boulders have been equipped with lips but not noses or eyes.

Avoiding Deep Nick of Dromore

From here, the waymarked Mountain End Path avoids the interesting but slightly challenging Deep Nick. To rejoin that path, head back away from the cliffs, north, for 50 metres to a waymark post. The small path heads downhill, northwest, towards the top of plantations. It bends left to bypass the north end of the Deep Nick of Dromore, before heading back uphill southwest, rather boggy and invisible, to regain the crest of the clints.

From the *Hush* sculpture, head west along the top edge of the cliffs, with views down to Dromore, to reach the high point 'Clint Eastward' at 243m. Ahead now is a deep notch, the Deep Nick of Dromore, which is a bit craggy on the descent.

From the very highest point of the clint, head down northwest for a few steps to the top of a small but wide granite slab. Head down to the left of this, then edge back below it, to reach a slanting terrace of grass and heather. Head left down this, southwest, with slabby rocks above and below. Keep down the same line, taking an occasional handhold on rocks among the heather, to the inner end of a level spur just below. At this gentler ground, turn down to the right into the bottom of the Deep Nick.

Pass left of the small pool, and zigzag up the broken slope opposite, zigging up to the right to start with, to reach 'Clint Westward'. Continue westwards along the top of the moor, soon with the waymark posts of the path (such as it is) seen on your right. Cross a soggy saddle for the slight rise to Mountain End (**294m**), the final and highest point of the clints. A waymark post stands just short of the summit.

Mountain End Path

As a quick route back from here, you could descend directly southwest to another waymark post on the open slopes below. A quad-bike track leads back below the clints and above **Russon Burn** to rejoin the railbed track.

From Mountain End, head northwest to remain on the moorland plateau, then bend west and only very slightly downhill to the highest point of a crossing fence. Aim for a junction with a fence heading away beyond: there's a stile at this point.

Continue southwest, on a faint grassland path to the left of the fence. As you approach the top of **Craig Hill**, ease up left to find a quad-bike track along the wide crest to the low summit cairn of lichened granite.

Culcronchie Hill is 10m lower than Craig Hill. This removes even the most tenuous pretence that it needs to be visited. But it's a pleasant grassy wander, with a quad-bike track winding among the occasional scattered granite boulders, and all overlooked by the Door of Cairnsmore, the great end wall of the granite mountain. Continue west, rejoining the fence, to a gate in a crossing wall. Head to the right, northwest, for a few steps to pick up the start of the quad-bike track. Follow it over the first two low humps, then to the slightly lower final one, which has **Culcronchie Hill**'s cairn, and a wide view westwards to the Cree estuary.

Return to **Craig Hill**. Quad-bike wheelmarks lead south, down a gentle grassy spur. Below the 300m contour, the slope gets steeper, with rather rough, tussocky grass. Head downhill to the former railway line that crosses the foot of the slope. Turn left along it; slightly raised where you meet it, it then passes through a soggy cutting to the edge of plantations. Continue ahead for 50 metres to cross a stream. ◄ Immediately across the stream, turn off right, between stream and plantations, to the nearby road.

Turn left for 1.5km. At a road junction and **New Rusko** house, the tarmac driveway to Dromore is ahead, but turn left signposted as a path to Mossdale, then right on a firm track following the railbed. This is the former

The railbed ahead looks like smooth walking, but it is blocked by swamps, willow scrub and broom bushes.

ROUTE 31 – CLINTS OF DROMORE

Gatehouse Station, featured in John Buchan's 1915 thriller *The Thirty-Nine Steps*. Soon, there is open pastureland to the right of the track. In another 800 metres, the trees end on the left as well, and the Mountain End Path arrives on the left just after a gate on the right. Through this gate, the Inbye Path is wide and green down the pastureland, bending away left then doubling back right to a new footbridge over Russon Burn, before it meets the tarmac lane below. Turn left to the visitor centre and car park at **Dromore**.

THE CLINTS OF DROMORE

A clint is a hummock of bare rock. At Dromore, the clints are the southern edge of the granite, which resisted the glacier better than the greywacke country rock that the farm and railway line are on.

The two highest clints lie on either side of a steep-sided gap, the Deep Nick of Dromore, which is a meltwater channel, where a river came tumbling off the side of a glacier. From the slightly lower 'Clint Westward', you can look back and admire the craggy 'Clint Eastward', from which the famously rugged Hollywood star of *A Fistful of Dollars* and *The Eiger Sanction* did not take his name.

The clints offer slabby granite at gentle angles, with plenty of scrambling opportunities, and are used by climbers from local outdoor centres. For climbers, there are restrictions during the bird nesting season from 15 February to 30 June. (For details, contact Scottish Natural Heritage/Cairnsmore of Fleet National Nature Reserve office: tel 01557 814435.)

Clints of Dromore

ROUTE 32
Knockman Wood

Start/finish	King Street, Newton Stewart (NX 409 662)
Alternative Start/finish	Minnigaff Church (NX 410 666)
Distance	10.5km (6½ miles)
Ascent	200m (700ft)
Harshness	1
Approx time	3hr
Terrain	Good paths and tracks, short soggy section on track to Garlies Castle
Highest point	Chambered cairn, 150m
Parking	Street parking in King Street, the A714 road running out of Newton Stewart towards Girvan
Variants	Leave out Garlies Castle, saving 3km (45min)
Note	In autumn 2018 the footbridge over River Cree was closed for repairs – if this should happen again, use alternative start at Minnigaff Church

The Wood of Cree is a series of old oakwoods, with an ambitious plan to rejoin them into a continuous squirrel-run from Newton Stewart to Loch Trool. As well as the woodland, this walk takes in an ancient cairn, remains of a medieval settlement and a ruined castle.

About 500 metres north along King Street from the Cree Bridge, a footpath sign (on the west side of the road) points across into a residential side street. Enter this between two concrete posts with balls on them and follow it to its end. Keep ahead into a small riverside park and a tarmac path to a high suspension bridge (footbridge) across **River Cree**. ◀

You can also reach the footbridge by turning off King Street 400 metres north of the footpath sign into an unsigned lane behind a phone box and pillar box.

Cross the bridge and the street beyond to a gate onto a path above Penkiln Burn. Follow it upstream briefly, then through the old churchyard of **Minnigaff Church**. Pass to the right of the church into a lane. ◀ In 100 metres, bear left on the main lane. In 800 metres, the lane

Car park opposite this point (alternative Start/finish).

ROUTE 32 – KNOCKMAN WOOD

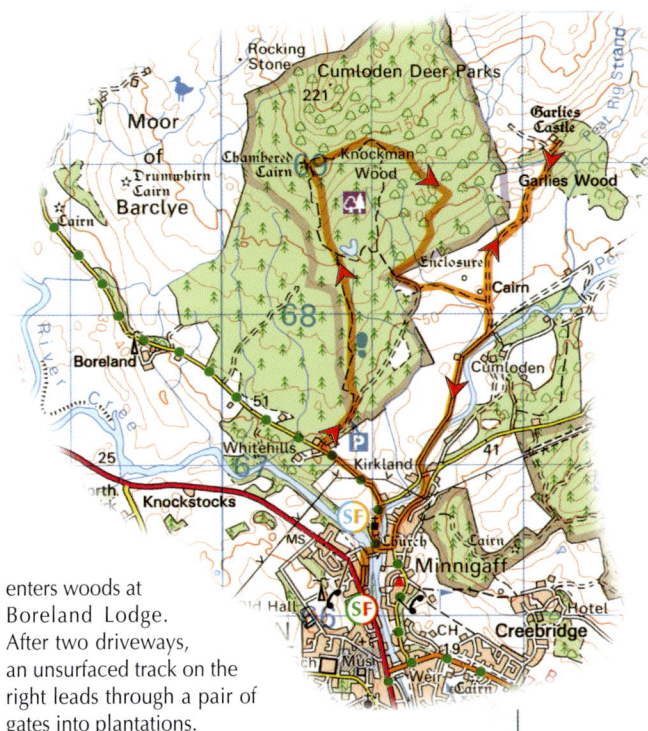

enters woods at Boreland Lodge. After two driveways, an unsurfaced track on the right leads through a pair of gates into plantations.

In 400 metres, you pass a **car park**; at once fork left through a gate. After 800 metres, the track passes through a wall into ground where plantations have been felled leaving a few remaining trees, mainly oaks, and regenerating scrub. As the track bends right, keep ahead in a good path, waymarked in three colours (blue, yellow and very faded red). The path crosses a track to a junction where the blue path departs to the right. ▶ Keep ahead, north, with yellow and red waymarks.

The path climbs gently into beautiful old oakwoods. In the clearing to the left of the path appears a very large **chambered cairn**, deeply lichened.

You could follow it for 100 metres to a pool, but that won't become a lovely spot until trees have regrown.

Chambered cairn, Knockman Wood

Boreland Chambered Cairn is a Bronze Age long cairn. No chambers are visible in this 'chambered cairn' – you can see a remnant of cairn chambers in Route 33 – but there are two large entrance boulders (or orthostats). Similar cairns have contained cremated human remains and pottery.

Opposite the chambered cairn, the path bends right, into the wood and up a slight rise to a path junction. Keep ahead, on the yellow trail. ◀ The grassy path runs gently downhill, with views across the woodland to Cairnsmore of Fleet. The very pleasant path runs east, southeast and then southwest, to arrive at a clearing with a high stone wall below it.

The red trail on the left is a through route to the Barclye Trails car park, Route 33.

Beside the track is a well-like cavity: this was a drying kiln for corn, part of the **Pheasant Liggat fermtoun** or medieval settlement. Beyond the next gate is more of the fermtoun, building remains and a noticeboard; the tall wall dividing it is the boundary of a Victorian deer park.

The blue trail joins from the right over a stout footbridge, and the combined path passes out of the woods by a gate. The wide green path runs along the plantation edge. After 150 metres, leave the waymarked trail through a field gate on the left for a faint green track across open moorland. This runs south of east for 600 metres, to join a rather clearer track, the junction marked by a hawthorn tree. ◀

Turn right here for the shortcut omitting Garlies Castle.

ROUTE 32 – KNOCKMAN WOOD

Turn back sharp left, north. The rough track is rather soggy and muddy for a few hundred metres across flat land, then bends right on firmer ground with the deer park wall over to its left. The track bends left through a gate in the tall wall. After another gate and a culvert over a stream, it rises up the wooded Castle Brae to the ruins of **Garlies Castle**.

> **Garlies Castle** is almost overwhelmed by ash trees, nettles and dog's mercury. But the interior still shows remains of a carved fireplace (you might make out the Stewart arms, and a stag hunt) and a stairway that was within the thickness of the outer wall. The main keep dates from around 1500, a stronghold of the Earls of Galloway (Clan Stewart).

Return along the rough track and keep ahead at the junction with hawthorn tree. The track joins a firmer one at the edge of trees hiding **Cumloden** house. Keep ahead as the track becomes tarmac after a small lodge house. The track runs beside **Penkiln Burn**, then across fields, then again beside the large stream. At Waukmill, the start of the public road, cross the old Queen Mary's Bridge and follow the lane to the left of the burn into the edge of **Minnigaff**. After 600 metres, turn right, to the footbridge over River Cree near the start of the walk. ▶

To return to the alternative start point, take a gate on the right above Penkiln Burn to pass through the churchyard.

Corn kiln, Pheasant Liggat

ROUTE 33
The Thieves Stones

Start/finish	Barclye Trails RSPB car park (NX 386 694)
Distance	11km (7 miles)
Ascent	300m (1000ft)
Harshness	2
Approx time	3hr 15min
Terrain	Tracks, and some rough grassy moorland
Highest point	Nappers Hill, 310m
Parking	The car park is on the Water of Cree road on the east side of River Cree. It is 1.5km south of the Wood of Cree car park, and is on the east (uphill) side of the road.

This walk and the previous one may seem rather similar – both are 3hr walks with archaeology. In the previous walk, the archaeology was in the woods; this time it's on the open moor. And while the previous walk's chambered cairn was more or less intact, this one's been dismantled to show you traces of the actual chambers. The walk also features a pair of standing stones and some wide views.

Follow the road northwards for 300 metres, to cross a small stream, then turn right up the tarmac driveway of Drannandow Farm. The driveway runs up through beautiful woodland. At the top of the woods, pass a house on the right, then fork right through a gate onto a faint green track (at the time of writing it has a caravan parked on it). After another gate, the track becomes clearer, bending left above **Drannandow Farm**.

Keep ahead across a stream and through a gate. The track turns uphill (northeast) between gorse bushes, with trees and a stream to its right. After another gate it crosses open field, and goes through two more gates to a track junction.

ROUTE 33 – THE THIEVES STONES

Between the two branches of the track, keep ahead up open rough moorland, parallel with a fence that's about 50 metres to your right. The moor is sprinkled with small rocks, often in arrangements that seem artificial. ▶ After 300 metres you reach the first archaeological remain, a low Bronze Age **cairn**. It's mostly grassed over, with stones showing at the top. Turn directly uphill, northeast, passing to the right of a small outcrop. The two Thieves Stones can be seen ahead by the sharp eyed. After 600 metres you reach a new fence. Cross it carefully at a strainer post (a thicker supporting post) to the two **Thieves Stones** just beyond. ▶

This moor was settled during prehistory through to the Middle Ages.

You could now shortcut down to the chambered cairn at Nappers Cottage – contour southeast then home in on the ruined cottage.

The two **Thieves Stones** are over 2m high. They may be the survivors of a stone circle. The name supposedly records the execution of two 13th-century cattle thieves or reivers – although hanging from trees was the convenient way of dealing with those guys.

Follow the fence east of north across the brow of the moor, crossing a side fence at its beginning. With felled plantation on the other side of the fence, slant slightly away from it, contouring so as to stay above rushes and

The Thieves standing stones

Larg Hill from Nappers Hill track

tussocks, to join the track seen ahead. It runs up through a gate in a wall and zigzags up the back of **Nappers Hill**, with views to Larg Hill. Then the track dips to a gate into plantations.

> Felling is taking place here until about 2020. If a sign on the gate discourages access, you can follow the plantation edge back south across Nappers, a gentle hill generously sprinkled with small rocks.

The track leads down through the plantation, much of it now clear-felled. Ignore a wide side track on the left and follow the smaller track ahead; it eventually bends right to leave the plantation at another gate. In 400 metres, it passes through another gate just above the derelict **Nappers Cottage**. Immediately through the gate, turn down left to a chambered cairn.

Many of the stones of the **Nappers chambered cairn** have been removed, presumably ending in nearby drystane dykes (drystone walls). This has exposed traces of three of the burial chambers inside it. The roofing has gone but some of the slabby stones of floors and side walls can be seen.

ROUTE 33 – THE THIEVES STONES

Return to the track and follow it downhill, with gates as it enters and then leaves a clear-felled plantation. The track bends to the left. As it starts to bend back right, leave it straight ahead up a knoll, passing the scattered remains of what looks like a former long house to another Bronze Age **cairn** on the knoll top.

Northeast of the cairn, a **stone circle** is shown on the map, 100 metres back towards the track. However, in my book, to count as a stone circle it has to have more than one stone... Authorities identify five of the rocks lying around here as belonging to the stone circle, but it's a very wide one and there are many other adventitious rocks as well. So this is the walk's least impressive ancient remain.

Continue down the track, soon passing through a gate and then rejoining the outward route above **Drannandow Farm** to return to the **car park**.

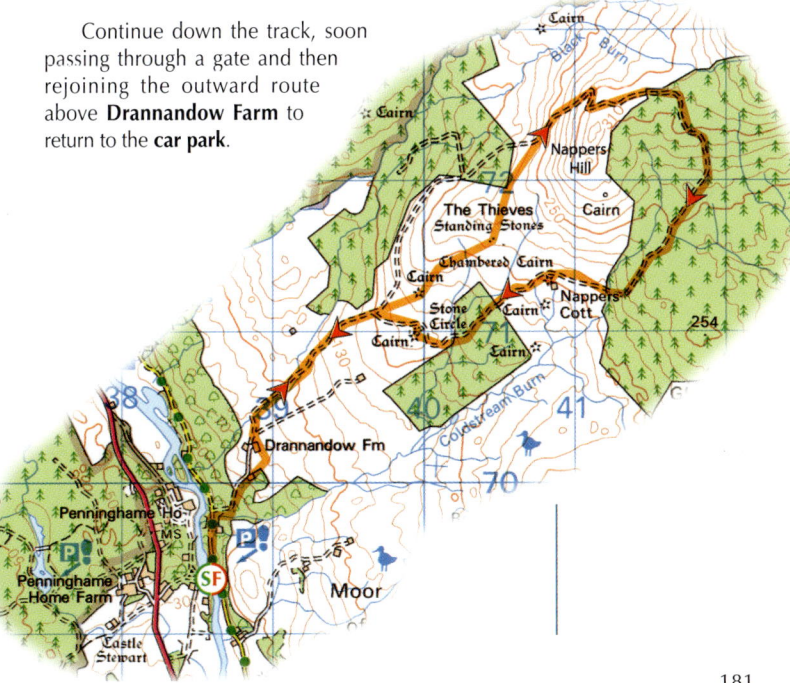

WALKING THE GALLOWAY HILLS

ROUTE 34
Wood of Cree

Start/finish	Wood of Cree car park (NX 381 708)
Distance	3.5km (2¼ miles)
Ascent	150m (500ft)
Harshness	1
Approx time	1hr 30min
Terrain	Paths, sometimes quite steep or quite faint
Highest point	Cordorcan, 130m
Parking	Wood of Cree RSPB car park on the Water of Cree road (east side of River Cree). This is 1.5km north of the Barclye Trails car park, and is on the west (riverbank) side of the road.
Variants	You can shortcut to the descending path halfway up

A short but quite steep waymarked walk up a stream with little waterfalls and through some ancient woodland – and if your feet are still itchy you can head down the road to Route 33.

Unless you're here very early, the short path from the car park to River Cree for the otter hide is best taken at the end of the walk. Any otters are less unlikely at dawn and dusk than during the middle of the day.

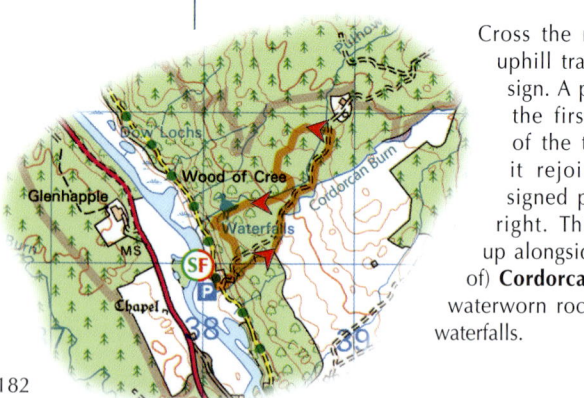

Cross the road into an uphill track with path sign. A path shortcuts the first wide bend of the track. Where it rejoins above, a signed path forks off right. This path runs up alongside (to the left of) **Cordorcan Burn**, with waterworn rocks and small waterfalls.

ROUTE 34 – WOOD OF CREE

Cordorcan Burn small waterfall

The slope eases, with the burn no longer a little gorge, and there's now an old wall between the path and the burn. At 500 metres from the car park, the path rejoins the earthen track. ▶ In another 200 metres, a path contouring left is signed as the Woodland Walk.

A sign indicates the short return to the car park back down the track.

Woodland Walk
This shorter Woodland Walk (1.5km) gives you just the waterfalls and the beauty of the oak trees. Take the side path (blue waymarks) contouring through trees for 200 metres and across a stout footbridge to meet the longer path as it descends.

The longer scrubland version ahead adds some regenerating woodland that is even better for birdlife. However, the scrubland is not so attractive in itself, and its vigorous regeneration means it no longer offers views across the Cree into the wilds of Wigtownshire. The track continues gently uphill, through mixed woodland, for 500 metres. With a patch of 'treated' (ie slaughtered) pines on your right, the signed path turns off to the left. ◄ The path is grassy and quite faint. It runs roughly west, crossing a footbridge, and passing a large granite boulder (glacial erratic) and two benches before dipping to cross another footbridge.

> The dead pines are for the benefit of woodpeckers.

The path descends roughly south through small trees and clearings. After going through a gap in a wall, it re-enters the mature oakwoods. It runs down as a hollowed path briefly, then to the right of a stream. The shorter Woodland Walk joins over a footbridge from the left, then the path itself crosses by a lower footbridge. It runs high above the small stream then descends steps to a small knoll, a former viewpoint. Like many woodland outlooks, this is no longer a view over the trees but a view of them, close-up. You can look over the canopy at the butterflies, if any. But greater Wigtownshire is no longer available for viewing.

The path rambles to the left through the wood, to join the track above the car park. Turn down to the right, soon passing the turn-off of the upward walk, to regain the **car park**.

Wood of Cree

SECTION 6: EXPEDITIONS

Heading down Cairnsgarroch, to Meaul

INTRODUCTION

The Galloway Hills are the largest patch of rugged country south of the Highlands. The Southern Uplands as a whole are lonely and unfrequented; Galloway is not only lonely, but also lovely. As elsewhere in the Southern Uplands, there will be no streetlight, no car headlight, not even the flickering torch of some other camper away on the other side of the glen. But only Galloway gives also the jagged shape of Curleywee or Craignaw against the black sky, the starlight reflected in the 20 bays of Loch Enoch. Not to mention that Galloway's shaggy tussocks make a uniquely comfortable sleeping surface.

These hills are remarkably tough and rugged for their size, as well as being reasonably accessible but also unknown to most long-distance enthusiasts. So they have been a regular locale for mountain marathons like the Original Mountain Marathon (OMM), formerly the Karrimor. They are indeed an exciting and challenging place for two-day or three-day expeditions with bivvybag or lightweight tent. Overnights alongside Loch Enoch are idyllic; or on still summer nights, when the midges are out, take to the heights of Tarfessock, Craignaw or Curleywee. And if the weather turns stormy (yes, Galloway has heavy rainfall, and the midges can be fierce as well), note the network of bothies described in Appendix B.

Any energetic person seeking a truly upland crossing of the long Southern Upland range will want to travel westwards, so as to have the Galloways as the grand climax after the gentler grassy going of the eastern and central summits. Route 35 could well be the finale of such a 'Not the Southern Upland Way' line. Alternatively, it's a freestanding three-dayer in its own right, linking Sanquhar and Bargrennan by a high and wild line.

For many years, a small band of local enthusiasts have enjoyed a variety of energetic outings: the rugged ground found on leaving the main ridgelines is training for anything that bigger and more celebrated hills can offer. Brief outlines are given for a couple of these, along with a classic circuit used as a bivvybag two-dayer by members of the Long Distance Walkers Association, and a purely literary trip inspired by *The Thirty-Nine Steps*.

ROUTE 35
Not the Southern Upland Way

Start	Sanquhar Tolbooth Museum (NS 780 099)
Finish	Bargrennan (NX 349 764)
Distance	82km (53 miles)
Ascent	3100m (10,500ft)
Harshness	4
Approx time	27hr (3 days' walking)
Terrain	Much pathless ground, with the first half to Carsphairn mostly gently grassy, and the second part to Loch Trool being rougher; easy finish along the Southern Upland Way
Highest point	Corserine, 814m
Facilities	One bothy on the route and another close alongside; café, B&Bs and some supplies at Carsphairn

The Southern Upland Way (SUW) lives up to its name by crossing at hilltop level – except here, in the range's finest section. Through the Galloway Hills, the SUW takes an ignoble low-level line along a foresters' gravel road – with, until patchy clear-felling started around 2010, views not of fine granite hills but of future loo rolls in the shape of spruce trees.

An alternative 'Not the SUW', travelling east to west, could start at St Abb's Head for some fine coastal walking to Pease Bay. Along Ettrick, it would take the high ridgeline north of the glen, continuing over Croft Head on the SUW's new higher line. From Beattock, it would take a more direct line to Wanlockhead over Queensberry to Durisdeer, and through the Enterkin Pass; before descending in high anticipation to Sanquhar. Now read on…

Leave Sanquhar southwest across a field to River Nith. Turn upstream to the Nith Bridge and turn left to Euchanfoot. A lovely riverside path leads up to the tiny Euchan glen road. Head up it past Old Barr, and take the second track descending left to cross **Euchan Water**.

WALKING THE GALLOWAY HILLS

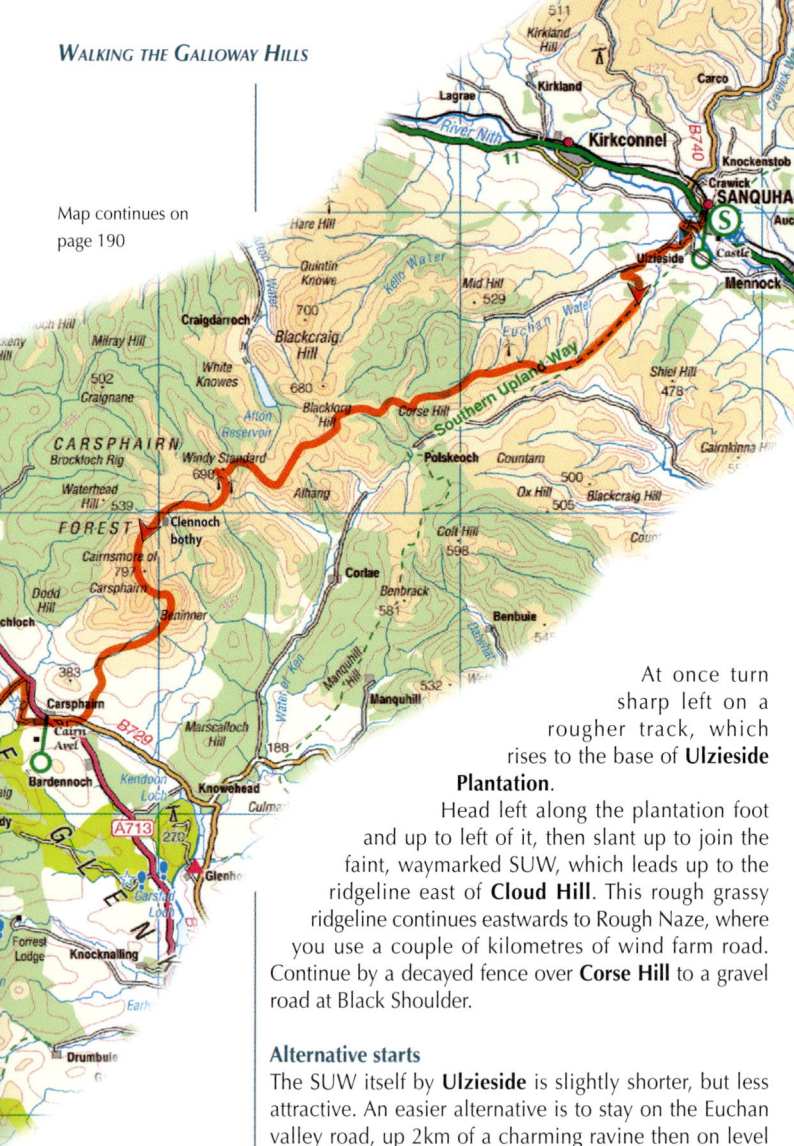

Map continues on page 190

At once turn sharp left on a rougher track, which rises to the base of **Ulzieside Plantation**.

Head left along the plantation foot and up to left of it, then slant up to join the faint, waymarked SUW, which leads up to the ridgeline east of **Cloud Hill**. This rough grassy ridgeline continues eastwards to Rough Naze, where you use a couple of kilometres of wind farm road. Continue by a decayed fence over **Corse Hill** to a gravel road at Black Shoulder.

Alternative starts

The SUW itself by **Ulzieside** is slightly shorter, but less attractive. An easier alternative is to stay on the Euchan valley road, up 2km of a charming ravine then on level

ROUTE 35 – NOT THE SOUTHERN UPLAND WAY

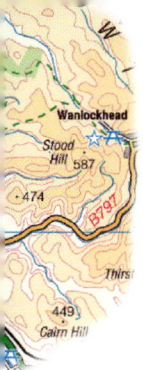

valley floor. Continue on forestry tracks past **Euchanhead** ruin to the valley head.

From Black Shoulder, a gravel track leads along **Ryegrain Rig**, then there's easy grassy going over **Meikledodd Hill**, **Alwhat** and **Alhang**. In the next rough col, the head of Holm Burn is a reliable water source before the stiffer climb to **Windy Standard**, Southern Scotland's oldest windfarm.

You arrive at the southeast end of the plateau. You could trek 500 metres between the turbines to visit the trig point, before heading with relief down south past the Deil's Putting Stone (a greywacke erratic boulder) and over Keoch Rig to **Clennoch bothy**. ▶

Immediately behind the bothy, cross the valley floor to the right of a broken wall and ascend **Cairnsmore of Carsphairn**. Descend (as Route 19) over **Beninner** and **Knockwhirn**. A rough track leads south to **Knockgray** and the B729, with a path beside the A713 into **Carsphairn**. ▶

Take a track west (still Route 19) to Water of Deugh and head upstream to rejoin the A713. Use fragments of old road on the left to the track foot near **Green Well of Scotland**. Follow Route 18 onto **Meaul** (or reverse it past the Garryhorn mines onto Coran of Portmark), and follow the ridge south to **Corserine** (now on Route 17).

Sanquhar to Clennoch bothy 28km (17½ miles) with 1000m (3300ft) ascent – about 9hr.

Clennoch bothy to Carsphairn 11.5km (7 miles) with 500m (1700ft) ascent – about 4hr.

Clennoch bothy and Cairnsmore of Carsphairn

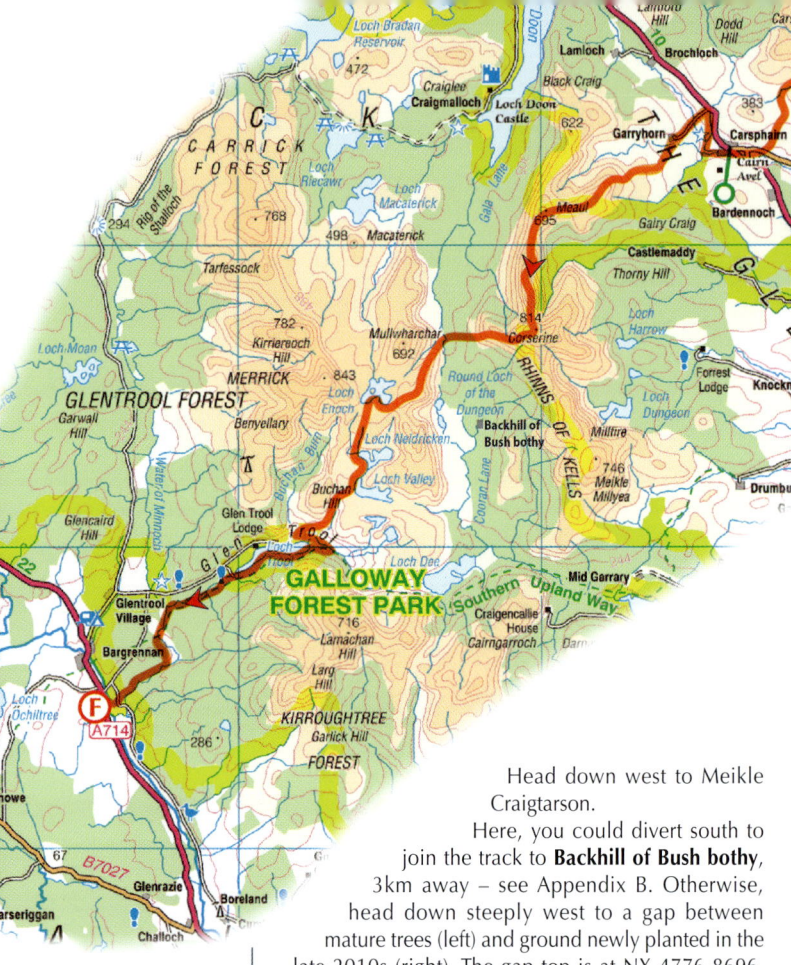

Carsphairn to forest road above Gala Lane 16.5km (10 miles) with 950m (3200ft) ascent – about 6hr.

Head down west to Meikle Craigtarson.

Here, you could divert south to join the track to **Backhill of Bush bothy**, 3km away – see Appendix B. Otherwise, head down steeply west to a gap between mature trees (left) and ground newly planted in the late 2010s (right). The gap top is at NX 4776 8696. A tough descent through the tree gap leads to a pair of forest roads. ◄

Go straight over the two joined forest roads into the continuing tree gap. Cross the stream that's the top of Gala Lane. Head up the Brishie ridge and cross Dungeon Hill to Craignairny – or in dry seasons, head up bare rock beside Pulskaig Burn to **Loch Enoch**.

ROUTE 35 – NOT THE SOUTHERN UPLAND WAY

Erratic granite boulder standing on hornfels, Buchan Hill; Merrick's ice-carved Gloon corrie above

From here, the ambitious could continue over either Craignaw or even Merrick. But the natural line is to follow a small path along the southern shore of the loch, and continue by Route 6 (the Three Lochs) down past **Loch Neldricken** and **Loch Valley**, to reach the track above **Loch Trool** at Buchan house, just down to the east of Bruce's Stone roadhead. ▶

Turn left, to the bridge over Glenhead Burn above the loch. Across the bridge, turn right on the SUW for its lovely section along the south side of **Loch Trool** and then down along the Waters of Trool and Minnoch and upstream by Water of Cree to **Bargrennan**. ▶

Gala Lane to Loch Trool 10.5km (6½ miles) with 400m (1300ft) ascent – about 4hr 30min.

Loch Trool at Buchan to Bargrennan 15km (9½ miles) with 250m (800ft) ascent – about 4hr.

OTHER ROUTES

THE THREE RIDGES

**Start/finish: Bruce's Stone, Loch Trool (NX 415 803);
Distance: 64km (40 miles); Ascent: 3500m (11,500ft)**
The Minnigaff, Rhinns of Kells and Awful Hand ranges make a natural circuit of about 65–70km (40–45 miles) depending on minor hills included. It's a magnificent natural line which can be (and has been!) achieved by strong runners or walkers in a long summer's day, or else treated as a three-day backpacking trip. Bruce's Stone at Loch Trool is the natural start point. The principal summits are Lamachan Hill, Curleywee, Millfore, Meikle Millyea, Corserine, Carlin's Cairn, Coran of Portmark, Shiel Hill, Craigmasheenie, Shalloch on Minnoch, Kirriereoch Hill, Merrick, and Benyellary.

The three ridge tops give pleasant and enjoyable walking (or running). However, the descent off Millfore by Cairnsgarroch is very tough, as is an ascent onto the Rhinns by Darrou. Coming off the north end, Route 17 (reversed) gives a comfortable line, with short cuts through the plantations being arduous and prickly. At the north end of the Awful Hand, ground onto and over Shiel Hill and Craigmasheenie is also demanding.

Support points are available at Black Water of Dee (16km); Carrick Lane, Loch Doon (39km); Ballochbeatties (50km).

GATEHOUSE TO GIRVAN

**Start: Gatehouse of Fleet (NX 598 562); Finish: Girvan pier (NX 179 983); Distance; 84km (52½ miles);
Ascent: 4400m (18,000ft)**
These two towns can be linked in a natural coast to coast across the Galloway peninsular, at about 84km (52

Whiteside Hill wind farm on the first stage of Route 35

miles). The crossings of Cairnsmore of Fleet, Curleywee, Craignaw, Merrick and Shalloch are complemented by smaller hills at either end, the Ayrshire ones being comfortably grassy. The principal summits are Bennan, Clints of Dromore, Cairnsmore of Fleet, Millfore, Curleywee, Craiglee, Craignaw, Merrick, Kirriereoch Hill, Shalloch on Minnoch, Craigenreoch, Auchensoul Hill, Troweir Hill and Saugh Hill.

Support points are available at Gatehouse Station (10.5km); Murray's Monument (25km); Straiton road (56km); Nick of the Balloch (60km); Barr village (71.5km); Tormitchell 77km.

THE FOUR CORBETTS

Start: Craigengillan, Water of Ken (NX 636 947); Finish: Stinchar Bridge (NX 395 956); Distance: 42.5km (26½ miles); Ascent; 2500m (8200ft)

The crossing of Cairnsmore of Carsphairn, Corserine, Merrick and Shalloch is a winter challenge (snow must be lying along the shores of Loch Enoch) for a pair of runners – or an inspiring long walk at any time. Additional hills Beninner and (after Carsphairn) Cairnsgarroch or else Coran of Portmark, along with Meaul and Carlin's

Cairn, should be included. The principal summits are Beninner, Cairnsmore of Carsphairn, Cairnsgarroch, Carlin's Cairn, Corserine, Merrick, Kirriereoch Hill, Shalloch on Minnoch, and a support point is available at Green Well of Scotland (12.5km).

The going on either side of Gala Lane is harsh, but given decent snow, the rest is reasonably runnable. The sudden arrival at Loch Enoch can be a most thrilling moment. Thoughts about avalanche possibilities or crampon requirement should be given to the steep descent off Kirriereoch Hill in particular. For the ambitious, the record stands at 7hr 5min (Duggie Gillespie and Colin Butler, February 2001).

STEPS FROM THE THIRTY-NINE STEPS

Start: Gatehouse Station below Cairnsmore of Fleet (NX 545 624); Finish: House o' Hill, near Glentrool Village (NX 350 769); Distance: 37km (23 miles); Ascent: 1800m (6000ft)

Richard Hannay, pursued by a gang of Sinister Foreigners and also by the Police, fixes on Galloway as the best place to go. John Buchan's thriller of 1915 has Hannay leaping off an early-morning train at 'a little place whose name I scarcely noted, set right in the heart of a bog' – this has to be the former Gatehouse Station below Cairnsmore of Fleet. From there, he sets off into the hills, occasionally pursued by a small 1914-model monoplane.

Little Spear and Merrick make the final big climb on the 'Three Ridges' expedition (Routes 11–12)

All we know about the pub at the end point is that it stands alone, and has a river bridge beside it. It has been identified as the House o' Hill, at Bargrennan – one of Buchan's ancestors lies in the kirkyard there. However, the hill trek occupies just five vivid paragraphs in Chapter 3, without enough detail to tie down any specific route or end point. (Hannay descends *eastwards* off the hill ridge, which would rule out the House o' Hill in the actual Galloway.)

One guidebook, while mentioning the House o' Hill, points out that it is not possible to reach it from Gatehouse Station in a single day's walking. For those who find such a statement an incitement to go out and do that very thing, a fine route suggests itself by Cairnsmore of Fleet and the west end of the Minnigaffs range. It would take in Clints of Dromore and Knee of Cairnsmore to cross A712 at Murray's Monument. Continue by Fell of Talnotry, Drigmorn and Pulnee Burn to skirt Curleywee, then over Lamachan Hill to descend by Caldons Burn to the Southern Upland Way. Finish, in the dark if necessary, by Stroan Bridge and Glentrool Village. The distance is 37km (23 miles) with 1800m of ascent (6000ft) – about 12 hours for a strong walker like Richard Hannay.

The appropriate walking kit will be a stout hazel stick, nailed boots, and a well-worn tweed suit. The principal summits are Cairnsmore of Fleet, Curleywee (bonus peak) and Lamachan Hill. A support point is available at A712 Murray's Monument (15km) (but Hannay just carried a packet of biscuits).

APPENDIX A
Route summary table

Route no	Route title	Distance	Ascent	Time	Harshness
Section 1: Glen Trool					
Route 1	Water of Minnoch and Glen Trool	13km (8 miles)	200m (600ft)	3hr 30min	1
Route 2	Water of Trool	7km (4½ miles)	150m (500ft)	2hr 15min	1
	variant: combine with Route 3	16.5km (10½ miles)	450m (1500ft)	5hr	1
	variant: combine with Routes 1 and 3	27.5km (17 miles)	650m (2100ft)	10hr	1
Route 3	Around Loch Trool	9.5km (6 miles)	300m (1000ft)	3hr	1
Route 4	Fell of Eschoncan to Bennan	7.5km (4½ miles)	450m (1500ft)	3hr 30min	4
	variant: short return by Culsharg bothy	4.5km (2½ miles)	250m (800ft)	2hr	4
	variant: continuation to Merrick	13.5km (8½ miles)	850m (2800ft)	5hr	4
	variant: on to Merrick and Loch Enoch	14.5km (9½ miles)	950m (3100ft)	6hr	4
Route 5	Merrick and Rig of the Buchan	13.5km (8½ miles)	900m (2900ft)	5hr 30min	3
Route 6	The Three Lochs	11.5km (7½ miles)	550m (1800ft)	4hr	3
Route 7	Craignaw	15.5km (9½ miles)	750m (2500ft)	6hr 30min	4
Route 8	Craiglee and Rig of the Jarkness	13.5km (8½ miles)	550m (1800ft)	5hr	5
Route 9	Mulldonoch to Curleywee	19.5km (12 miles)	950m (3200ft)	7hr 30min	4
	variant: combine Routes 8 and 9	23.5km (14½ miles)	1200m (4000ft)	9hr	5

Appendix A – Route summary table

Route no	Route title	Distance	Ascent	Time	Harshness
Route 10	Caldron of the Merrick	17km (10½ miles)	950m (3200ft)	7hr	5
Section 2: The Awful Hand					
Route 11	Kirriereoch Hill and Merrick	19km (12 miles)	900m (3000ft)	6hr 30min	3
	variant: finish over Benyellary	20km 12½ miles)	900m (3000ft)	7hr	3
Route 12	The Awful Hand: Shalloch to Benyellary	24km (15 miles)	1150m (3900ft)	8hr 30min	4
	variant: omit Shalloch	22km (13½ miles)	1000m (3400ft)	7hr 30min	4
Route 13	Shalloch on Minnoch	14.5km (9 miles)	650m (2100ft)	5hr	4
	variant: straight up-and-down of Shalloch	11.5km (7½ miles)	450m (1500ft)	3hr 45min	2
Route 14	Craigmasheenie and Shiel Hill	14km (8½ miles)	650m (2200ft)	5hr	5
	variant: Cornish Hill and Loch	5.5km (3½ miles)	150m (500ft)	1hr 45min	1
Section 3: Loch Doon					
Route 15	Craiglee of Doon	8km (5 miles)	400m (1300ft)	3hr 30min	5
Route 16	Hoodens Hill and Mullwharchar	24km (15 miles)	950m (3000ft)	7hr 30min	5
	variant: omit Dungeon Hill	21km (13 miles)	800m (2700ft)	6hr	5
	variant: combine Routes 16 and 17	32.5km (20½ miles)	1600m (5300ft)	11hr	5
Route 17	Northern Rhinns of Kells from Loch Doon	25.5km (16 miles)	1000m (3300ft)	8hr	4
Section 4: The Glenkens					
Route 18	Garryhorn and the northern Rhinns of Kells	16km (10 miles)	750m (2500ft)	5hr 30min	4
Route 19	Cairnsmore of Carsphairn	17km (10½ miles)	750m (2500ft)	5hr 45min	3

WALKING THE GALLOWAY HILLS

Route no	Route title	Distance	Ascent	Time	Harshness
	variant: down over Dunool	11.5km (7¼ miles)	650m (2200ft)	4hr	3
Route 20	Craig of Knockgray	7.5km (4½ miles)	200m (700ft)	2hr 15min	3
	variant: from Liggat	3.5km (2 miles)	200m (700ft)	1hr 15min	2
Route 21	Corserine from Forrest Lodge	14.5km (9 miles)	700m (2700ft)	5hr	4
Route 22	Southern Rhinns of Kells	19km (12 miles)	950m (3200ft)	8hr	3
	variant: Rhinns of Kells complete	29km (18 miles)	1300m (4400ft)	9hr 30min	4
Route 23	Mulloch Hill	5km (3¼ miles)	120m (400ft)	1hr 30min	1
Route 24	Waterside Hill	7km (4½ miles)	200m (700ft)	2hr 15min	2
	variant: combine Routes 24 and 25	12km (7½ miles)	350m (1100ft)	3hr 30min	3
Route 25	Dunveoch	7.5km (5 miles)	200m (700ft)	2hr 15min	3
Section 5: Talnotry and the south					
Route 26	Larg Hill to Curleywee	19km (12 miles)	850m (2800ft)	6hr 45min	3
	variant: continue over Millfore	21km (13 miles)	1100m (3700ft)	8hr	4
Route 27	Curleywee by Stronbae Hill	17km (10½ miles)	700m (2300ft)	5hr 45min	4
Route 28	Millfore	12km (7½ miles)	650m (2100ft)	4hr 30min	4
	variant: Murray's Monument short walk	3km (2 miles)	150m (500ft)	1hr	1
Route 29	Cairnsmore of Fleet from the north	14.5km (9 miles)	800m (2700ft)	6hr	5
Route 30	Cairnsmore of Fleet from the south	15km (9½ miles)	750m (2700ft)	5hr 15min	2

Appendix A – Route summary table

Route no	Route title	Distance	Ascent	Time	Harshness
Route 31	Clints of Dromore	13km (8 miles)	400m (1300ft)	4hr 30min	4
Route 32	Knockman Wood	10.5km (6½ miles)	200m (700ft)	3hr	1
	variant: without Garlies Castle	7.5km (4½ miles)	150m (500ft)	2hr 25min	1
Route 33	The Thieves Stones	11km (7 miles)	300m (1000ft)	3hr 15min	2
Route 34	Wood of Cree	3.5km (2¼ miles)	150m (500ft)	1hr 30min	1
Section 6: Expeditions					
Route 35	Not the Southern Upland Way	82km (53 miles)	3100m (10,500ft)	27hr (3 days)	4

APPENDIX B
The bothies

The five bothies are conveniently placed for exploration of all the Galloway ranges. Perhaps too conveniently – two of them are alongside forest tracks whose entry gates are usually not locked, and a third is beside the busy Merrick path: so they do get heavy use, especially at summer weekends, including from drinking parties. However, a stay can often be a very pleasant experience, particularly in the off-seasons. If Forestry and Land Scotland (formerly Forestry Commission) stick to their announced policy of locking gates along the access tracks, the condition of these bothies (especially Backhill and White Laggan) should improve: in the past they've suffered badly from rubbish and vandalism.

Three of the bothies are managed by the Mountain Bothies Association, with up-to-date details on their website.

Access routes from public transport stops are:

- *The most convenient:* From St John's Town of Dalry, the Southern Upland Way gives convenient access to **White Laggan** and **Backhill of Bush** bothies, especially as some SUW accommodation points in Dalry offer a vehicle drop-off at Mid Garrary above Clatteringshaws Loch.
- *The most exciting:* From the 520 bus stop at Green Well of Scotland, follow the northern Rhinns of Kells ridge to Corserine, and descend westwards to Meikle Craigtarson. From its tip, descend quite steeply just west of south, and pass down immediately to the right (west) of a large roadstone quarry to reach the forest track north of **Backhill of Bush**.
- *The prettiest:* From Bargrennan or Glentrool Village, use Southern Upland Way to **White Laggan**, or branch off at Caldons for **Culsharg**.
- *The inaccessible:* **Tunskeen** is not reachable from any bus stop. Get there from one of the other bothies!
- *The challenging exit:* With rucksacks lightened by having eaten all your food, head out from **White Laggan** over Millfore and/or Cairnsmore of Fleet for a triumphant descent to Newton Stewart.

White Laggan (MBA)
Extensively renovated in 2018. Sleeping accommodation is mostly on the floor. A good base for the Minnigaff Hills and the southern Rhinns of Kells.

Backhill of Bush
The Backhill is too readily available to 'drink and vandalism' visitors, and so is often found in very poor condition. From the bothy, forest tracks run up east to not far below the south end of the Corserine–Millfire saddle. (The path marked on Landranger maps

Appendix B — The bothies

Culsharg bothy, 2018

has gone.) Crossing Silver Flowe to the Dungeon range is awkward unless conditions are very dry.

Tunskeen (MBA)
The only Galloway Hills bothy not enclosed within plantations. It is well furnished, including a stove, and as comfortable as a bothy can be. It's reached from the Carrick Forest Drive, where there's a vehicle barrier on the branch track to the bothy.

Tunskeen offers access to Shalloch on Minnoch via its steep eastern slope, and to low but bouldery Macaterick, named after one of the lawless tribes of the 18th century. The obvious valley line south towards Loch Enoch is very, very tough.

Culsharg
The bothy has a fireplace but no sleeping platform (any wooden platform will have gone up the chimney as informal firewood). In 2018, the nice new windows had just been comprehensively smashed out.

Clennoch (MBA)
A charming and well-furnished bothy tucked away on the east side of Cairnsmore of Carsphairn, and offering an enjoyable outing onto that hill.

Lost bothies
The wigwam on the west slope of Tarfessock, and Shiel of Castlemaddy, west of Carsphairn, have both been removed.

APPENDIX C
Information points

Visitor information and accommodation
VisitScotland Dumfries
tel 01387 253862
www.visitscotland.com

www.newtonstewart.org

www.gallowayforestpark.com

Also see the Southern Upland Way website:
www.southernuplandway.gov.uk

Newton Stewart Walking Festival: second week in May, since 2003; walks in Galloway hills, surrounding countryside and coast:
www.walkfestnewtonstewart.com

Forestry and Land Scotland (formerly Forestry Commission)
forestryandland.gov.scot

Newton Stewart local office
tel 0300 067 6800
enquiries.south@forestryandland.gov.scot

For information about Dark Sky Park stargazing events search for Galloway International Dark Sky Park

Weather
Mountain Weather Information Service has a dedicated Southern Uplands page, usually with Galloway detail:
www.mwis.org.uk

Access
Galloway Forest Park, like the rest of Scotland, has open access right to roam (including wild camping). This right must be exercised responsibly – with consideration for land managers, other hillgoers, and the environment:
www.outdooraccess-scotland.scot

Mountain Rescue
In emergency, dial 999 and ask for Police Scotland, then Mountain Rescue. Galloway Mountain Rescue Team is based at Newton Stewart:
www.gallowaymrt.org.uk

NOTES

DOWNLOAD THE ROUTES IN GPX FORMAT

All the routes in this guide are available for download from:

www.cicerone.co.uk/1010/GPX

as standard format GPX files. You should be able to load them into most online GPX systems and mobile devices, whether GPS or smartphone. You may need to convert the file into your preferred format using a conversion programme such as gpsvisualizer.com or one of the many other such websites and programmes.

When you follow this link, you will be asked for your email address and where you purchased the guidebook, and have the option to subscribe to the Cicerone e-newsletter.

www.cicerone.co.uk

LISTING OF CICERONE GUIDES

BRITISH ISLES CHALLENGES, COLLECTIONS AND ACTIVITIES
Great Walks on the England Coast Path
Map and Compass
The Big Rounds
The Book of the Bivvy
The Book of the Bothy
The Mountains of England and Wales: Vol 1 Wales
Vol 2 England
The National Trails
Walking the End to End Trail

SHORT WALKS SERIES
Short Walks Hadrian's Wall
Short Walks Lake District — Keswick, Borrowdale and Buttermere
Short Walks Lake District — Windermere Ambleside and Grasmere
Short Walks Lake District — Coniston and Langdale
Short Walks in Arnside and Silverdale
Short Walks in Nidderdale
Short Walks in Northumberland: Wooler, Rothbury, Alnwick and the coast
Short Walks on the Malvern Hills
Short Walks in Cornwall: Falmouth and the Lizard
Short Walks in Cornwall: Land's End and Penzance
Short Walks in the South Downs: Brighton, Eastbourne and Arundel
Short Walks in the Surrey Hills
Short Walks on Dartmoor — South: Ivybridge and Princetown
Short Walks on Exmoor
Short Walks Winchester
Short Walks in Pembrokeshire: Tenby and the south
Short Walks in Dumfries and Galloway
Short Walks on the Isle of Mull
Short Walks on the Orkney Islands
Short Walks on the Shetland Islands

SCOTLAND
Ben Nevis and Glen Coe
Cycling in the Hebrides
Cycling the North Coast 500
Great Mountain Days in Scotland
Mountain Biking in Southern and Central Scotland
Mountain Biking in West and North West Scotland
Not the West Highland Way Scotland
Scotland's Best Small Mountains
Scotland's Mountain Ridges
Scottish Wild Country Backpacking
Skye's Cuillin Ridge Traverse
The Borders Abbeys Way
The Great Glen Way
The Great Glen Way Map Booklet
The Hebridean Way
The Hebrides
The Isle of Mull
The Isle of Skye
The Skye Trail
The Southern Upland Way
The West Highland Way
Walking Ben Lawers, Rannoch and Atholl
Walking in the Cairngorms
Walking in the Pentland Hills
Walking in the Scottish Borders
Walking in the Southern Uplands
Walking in Torridon, Fisherfield, Fannichs and An Teallach
Walking Loch Lomond and the Trossachs
Walking on Arran
Walking on Harris and Lewis
Walking on Jura, Islay and Colonsay
Walking on Rum and the Small Isles
Walking on the Orkney and Shetland Isles
Walking on Uist and Barra
Walking the Cape Wrath Trail
Walking the Corbetts Vol 1 South of the Great Glen
Walking the Corbetts Vol 2 North of the Great Glen
Walking the Fife Pilgrim Way
Walking the Galloway Hills
Walking the John o' Groats Trail
Walking the Munros
Vol 1 — Southern, Central and Western Highlands
Vol 2 — Northern Highlands and the Cairngorms
Walking the West Highland Way
West Highland Way Map Booklet
Winter Climbs in the Cairngorms
Winter Climbs: Ben Nevis and Glen Coe

NORTHERN ENGLAND ROUTES
Cycling the Reivers Route
Cycling the Way of the Roses
Hadrian's Cycleway
Hadrian's Wall Path
Hadrian's Wall Path Map Booklet
The Coast to Coast Cycle Route
The Coast to Coast Map Booklet
The Coast to Coast Walk
The Pennine Way
Pennine Way Map Booklet
Walking the Dales Way
The Dales Way Map Booklet

LAKE DISTRICT
Bikepacking in the Lake District
Cycling in the Lake District
Great Mountain Days in the Lake District
Joss Naylor's Lakes, Meres and Waters of the Lake District
Lake District Winter Climbs
Lake District: High Level and Fell Walks
Lake District: Low Level and Lake Walks
Mountain Biking in the Lake District
Outdoor Adventures with Children — Lake District
Scrambles in the Lake District
— North
South
Trail and Fell Running in the Lake District
Walking The Cumbria Way
Walking the Lake District Fells —
Borrowdale
Buttermere
Coniston
Keswick
Langdale
Mardale and the Far East
Patterdale
Wasdale
Walking the Tour of the Lake District

NORTH-WEST ENGLAND AND THE ISLE OF MAN
Cycling the Pennine Bridleway
Isle of Man Coastal Path
The Lancashire Cycleway
The Lune Valley and Howgills
Walking in Cumbria's Eden Valley
Walking in Lancashire
Walking in the Forest of Bowland and Pendle
Walking on the Isle of Man
Walking on the West Pennine Moors
Walking the Ribble Way
Walks in Silverdale and Arnside

NORTH-EAST ENGLAND, YORKSHIRE DALES AND PENNINES
Cycling in the Yorkshire Dales
Great Mountain Days in the Pennines
Mountain Biking in the Yorkshire Dales
The Cleveland Way and the Yorkshire Wolds Way
The Cleveland Way Map Booklet
The North York Moors
Trail and Fell Running in the Yorkshire Dales
Walking in County Durham
Walking in Northumberland
Walking in the North Pennines

Walking in the Yorkshire Dales:
  North and East
  South and West
Walking St Cuthbert's Way
Walking St Oswald's Way and Northumberland Coast Path

DERBYSHIRE, PEAK DISTRICT AND MIDLANDS
Cycling in the Peak District
Dark Peak Walks
Scrambles in the Dark Peak
Walking in Derbyshire
Walking in the Peak District —
  White Peak East
  White Peak West

WALES AND WELSH BORDERS
Cycle Touring in Wales
Cycling Lon Las Cymru
Great Mountain Days in Snowdonia
Hillwalking in Shropshire
Mountain Walking in Snowdonia
Offa's Dyke Path
Offa's Dyke Map Booklet
The Pembrokeshire Coast Path
Pembrokeshire Coast Path Map Booklet
Scrambles in Snowdonia
Snowdonia: 30 Low-level and Easy Walks — North, South
The Cambrian Way
The Snowdonia Way
The Wye Valley Walk
Walking Glyndwr's Way
Walking in Carmarthenshire
Walking in Pembrokeshire
Walking in the Brecon Beacons
Walking in the Wye Valley
Walking on Gower
Walking the Severn Way
Walking the Shropshire Way
Walking the Wales Coast Path

SOUTHERN ENGLAND
20 Classic Sportive Rides in South East England
20 Classic Sportive Rides in South West England
Cycling in the Cotswolds
Mountain Biking on the North Downs
Mountain Biking on the South Downs
The North Downs Way
North Downs Way Map Booklet
Walking the South West Coast Path
South West Coast Path Map Booklet — Vol 1: Minehead to St Ives
  — Vol 2: St Ives to Plymouth
  — Vol 3: Plymouth to Poole
Suffolk Coast and Heath Walks
The Cotswold Way
The Cotswold Way Map Booklet
The Kennet and Avon Canal
The Lea Valley Walk
The Peddars Way and Norfolk Coast Path
The Pilgrims' Way
The Ridgeway National Trail
The Ridgeway Map Booklet
The South Downs Way
The South Downs Way Map Booklet
The Thames Path
The Thames Path Map Booklet
The Two Moors Way
Two Moors Way Map Booklet
Walking Hampshire's Test Way
Walking in Cornwall
Walking in Essex
Walking in Kent
Walking in London
Walking in Norfolk
Walking in the Chilterns
Walking in the Cotswolds
Walking in the Isles of Scilly
Walking in the New Forest
Walking in the North Wessex Downs
Walking on Dartmoor
Walking on Guernsey
Walking on Jersey
Walking on the Isle of Wight
Walking the Dartmoor Way
Walking the Jurassic Coast
Walking the Sarsen Way
Walks in the South Downs National Park
Cycling Land's End to John o' Groats

ALPS CROSS-BORDER ROUTES
100 Hut Walks in the Alps
Alpine Ski Mountaineering Vol 1 — Western Alps
The Karnischer Hohenweg
The Tour of the Bernina
Trekking the Tour du Mont Blanc
Tour du Mont Blanc Map Booklet
Trail Running — Chamonix and the Mont Blanc region
Trekking Chamonix to Zermatt
Trekking in the Alps
Trekking in the Silvretta and Ratikon Alps
Trekking Munich to Venice
Walking in the Alps

FRANCE, BELGIUM, AND LUXEMBOURG
Camino de Santiago — Via Podiensis
Chamonix Mountain Adventures
Cycling London to Paris
Cycling the Canal de la Garonne
Cycling the Canal du Midi
Mont Blanc Walks
Mountain Adventures in the Maurienne
Short Treks on Corsica
The Grand Traverse of the Massif Central
The Moselle Cycle Route
Trekking in the Vanoise
Trekking the Cathar Way
Trekking the GR10
Trekking the GR20 Corsica
Trekking the Robert Louis Stevenson Trail
The GR5 Trail
The GR5 Trail — Vosges and Jura Benelux and Lorraine
Via Ferratas of the French Alps
Walking in Provence — East
Walking in Provence — West
Walking in the Auvergne
Walking in the Briançonnais
Walking in the Dordogne
Walking in the Haute Savoie: North
Walking in the Haute Savoie: South
Walking on Corsica
Walking the Brittany Coast Path
Walking in the Ardennes

PYRENEES AND FRANCE/SPAIN CROSS-BORDER ROUTES
Shorter Treks in the Pyrenees
The Pyrenean Haute Route
The Pyrenees
Trekking the Cami dels Bons Homes
Trekking the GR11 Trail
Walks and Climbs in the Pyrenees

SPAIN AND PORTUGAL
Camino de Santiago: Camino Frances
Costa Blanca Mountain Adventures
Cycling the Camino de Santiago
Mountain Walking in Mallorca
Mountain Walking in Southern Catalunya
Spain's Sendero Historico: The GR1
The Andalucian Coast to Coast Walk
The Camino del Norte and Camino Primitivo
The Camino Ingles and Ruta do Mar
The Mountains Around Nerja
The Mountains of Ronda and Grazalema
The Sierras of Extremadura
Trekking in Mallorca
Trekking in the Canary Islands
Trekking the GR7 in Andalucia
Walking and Trekking in the Sierra Nevada
Walking in Andalucia
Walking in Catalunya — Barcelona
  Girona Pyrenees
Walking in the Picos de Europa
Walking La Via de la Plata and Camino Sanabres
Walking on Gran Canaria

Walking on La Gomera and El Hierro
Walking on La Palma
Walking on Lanzarote and Fuerteventura
Walking on Tenerife
Walking on the Costa Blanca
Walking the Camino dos Faros
Portugal's Rota Vicentina
The Camino Portugues
Walking in Portugal
Walking in the Algarve
Walking on Madeira
Walking on the Azores

SWITZERLAND
Switzerland's Jura Crest Trail
The Swiss Alps
Tour of the Jungfrau Region
Trekking the Swiss Via Alpina
Walking in Arolla and Zinal
Walking in the Bernese Oberland — Jungfrau region
Walking in the Engadine — Switzerland
Walking in the Valais
Walking in Ticino
Walking in Zermatt and Saas-Fee

GERMANY
Hiking and Cycling in the Black Forest
The Danube Cycleway Vol 1
The Rhine Cycle Route
The Westweg
Walking in the Bavarian Alps

POLAND, SLOVAKIA, ROMANIA, HUNGARY AND BULGARIA
The Danube Cycleway Vol 2
The High Tatras
The Mountains of Romania

SCANDINAVIA, ICELAND AND GREENLAND
Hiking in Norway — North
Hiking in Norway — South
Trekking the Kungsleden
Trekking in Greenland — The Arctic Circle Trail
Walking and Trekking in Iceland

SLOVENIA, CROATIA, SERBIA, MONTENEGRO AND ALBANIA
Hiking Slovenia's Juliana Trail
Mountain Biking in Slovenia
The Islands of Croatia
The Julian Alps of Slovenia
The Mountains of Montenegro
The Peaks of the Balkans Trail
The Slovene Mountain Trail
Walking in Slovenia: The Karavanke
Walks and Treks in Croatia

ITALY
Alta Via 1 — Trekking in the Dolomites
Alta Via 2 — Trekking in the Dolomites
Day Walks in the Dolomites
Italy's Grande Traversata delle Alpi
Italy's Sibillini National Park
Ski Touring and Snowshoeing in the Dolomites
The Way of St Francis
Trekking Gran Paradiso: Alta Via 2
Trekking in the Apennines
Trekking the Giants' Trail: Alta Via 1 through the Italian Pennine Alps
Via Ferratas of the Italian Dolomites: Vol 1
Vol 2
Walking in Abruzzo
Walking in Italy's Cinque Terre
Walking in Italy's Stelvio National Park
Walking in Sicily
Walking in the Aosta Valley
Walking in the Dolomites
Walking in Tuscany
Walking in Umbria
Walking Lake Como and Maggiore
Walking Lake Garda and Iseo
Walking on the Amalfi Coast
Walking the Via Francigena Pilgrim Route — Part 2
Walking the Via Francigena Pilgrim Route — Part 3
Walks and Treks in the Maritime Alps

IRELAND
The Wild Atlantic Way and Western Ireland
Walking the Kerry Way
Walking the Wicklow Way

EUROPEAN CYCLING
Cycling the Route des Grandes Alpes
Cycling the Ruta Via de la Plata
The Elbe Cycle Route
The River Loire Cycle Route
The River Rhone Cycle Route

INTERNATIONAL CHALLENGES, COLLECTIONS AND ACTIVITIES
Europe's High Points
Walking the Via Francigena Pilgrim Route — Part 1

AUSTRIA
Innsbruck Mountain Adventures
Trekking Austria's Adlerweg
Trekking in Austria's Hohe Tauern
Trekking in Austria's Stubai Alps
Trekking in Austria's Zillertal Alps
Walking in Austria
Walking in the Salzkammergut: the Austrian Lake District

MEDITERRANEAN
The High Mountains of Crete
Trekking in Greece
Walking and Trekking in Zagori
Walking and Trekking on Corfu
Walking on the Greek Islands — the Cyclades
Walking in Cyprus
Walking on Malta

HIMALAYA
8000 metres
Everest: A Trekker's Guide
Trekking in the Karakoram

NORTH AMERICA
Hiking and Cycling the California Missions Trail
The John Muir Trail
The Pacific Crest Trail

SOUTH AMERICA
Aconcagua and the Southern Andes
Hiking and Biking Peru's Inca Trails
Trekking in Torres del Paine

AFRICA
Kilimanjaro
Walking in the Drakensberg
Walks and Scrambles in the Moroccan Anti-Atlas

NEW ZEALAND AND AUSTRALIA
Hiking the Overland Track

CHINA, JAPAN, AND ASIA
Annapurna
Hiking and Trekking in the Japan Alps and Mount Fuji
Hiking in Hong Kong
Japan's Kumano Kodo Pilgrimage
Japan's Kumano Kodo Pilgrimage
Trekking in Bhutan
Trekking in Ladakh
Trekking in Tajikistan
Trekking in the Himalaya

TECHNIQUES
Fastpacking
The Mountain Hut Book

MINI GUIDES
Alpine Flowers
Navigation
Pocket First Aid and Wilderness Medicine

MOUNTAIN LITERATURE
A Walk in the Clouds
Abode of the Gods
Fifty Years of Adventure
The Pennine Way — the Path, the People, the Journey
Unjustifiable Risk?

For full information on all our guides, books and eBooks, visit our website:
www.cicerone.co.uk

CICERONE

Trust Cicerone to guide your next adventure, wherever it may be around the world...

Discover guides for hiking, mountain walking, backpacking, trekking, trail running, cycling and mountain biking, ski touring, climbing and scrambling in Britain, Europe and worldwide.

Connect with Cicerone online and find inspiration.

- buy books and ebooks
- articles, advice and trip reports
- GPX files and updates
- regular newsletter

cicerone.co.uk